Walt Disney's
MICKEY MOUSE
IN COLOR

PANTHEON BOOKS/NEW YORK

Produced by **Another Rainbow Publishing, Inc.** Prescott, Ariz.

Dedicated with love to the memory of
Floyd Gottfredson
the man who gave us the greatest Mickey

Library of Congress Cataloging-in-Publication Data

Gottfredson, Floyd.
   Walt Disney's Mickey Mouse in color.
   Bibliography: p.
   1. Mickey Mouse (Cartoon character) 2. Walt Disney Company. I. Walt Disney Company. II. Title. III. Title: Mickey Mouse in color.
NC1766.U52D542   1988   741.5'09794'93   88-43087
ISBN 0-394-57519-9

Manufactured in the United States of America

First Edition

PRODUCTION STAFF

Editor: Bruce Hamilton

Associate Editors: Leonard (John) Clark
Byron Erickson

Contributing Editor: Geoffrey Blum

Art Director: Gary Leach

Production: Susan Daigle-Leach
Connie de Jong
Virginia Gibbons
Russ Miller

Contributors: Thomas Andrae
David R. Smith

Sunday page color based on the original color proofs. Mechanical separations by Visual Concepts, Inc.

Daily strips colored by Mike McCormick.
Full-color rendering by: Steve Oliff
Gloria Vásquez
Marie Vadon
Rueben Rude
Frisketter: Dustin Smith

Printed at Imperial Litho/Graphics, Phoenix, AZ.

Bound at H & H Bookbinding, Indianapolis, IN.

Acknowledgements

Murphy Anderson, Murphy Anderson, Jr., Joshua Arfer, Bill Armstrong, Garé Barks, Alberto Becattini, Bill Blackbeard, Luca Boschi, Karen Brower, Steve Carlson, David Cleghorn, Lee Clouse, Greg Crosby, Denis Dermody, Ginger Dickinson, Jessie Furby, Gary Gabner, Mike Glad, Mattie Gottfredson, Norman Gottfredson, Carl Grasso, Mark Hensley, Ted Hill, Doug Hindley, Wendall Mohler, Tina Moreland, Wayne Morris, Rose Motzko, High Nelson, Steve Oliff, Chris Rock, Cibylle Scheliga, Paula Sigman, David Smith, Jeanette Steiner, Lisa Stricklin, Klaus Strzyz, Robyn Tynan, Leslie Villegas, Wabash Sid, Jeff Walker, Malcolm Willits, Jay Willson

TABLE OF CONTENTS

Mickey's Second Father
Introduction by Geoffrey Blum 5

Of Mouse and the Man
Essay by Thomas Andrae 9

The Sundays by Floyd Gottfredson

"Rumplewatt the Giant" 37

"Dr. Oofgay's Secret Serum" 47

"The Case of the Vanishing Coats" 63

"The Robin Hood Adventure" 71

The Dailies by Floyd Gottfredson

The Man Who Drew the Mouse
Interview with Floyd Gottfredson by David R. Smith 97

"Blaggard Castle" 113

"Pluto and the Dogcatcher" 133

"The Mail Pilot" 137

"Mickey Mouse Outwits the Phantom Blot" 160

Indexing the Mouse
A Bibliography of Floyd Gottfredson's **Mickey Mouse** Adventures Stories 185

Floyd Gottfredson
in 1982 talking with
Donald Duck artist Carl Barks

MICKEY'S SECOND FATHER

An Introduction

Mickey Mouse is so roundly acknowledged as Walt Disney's offspring that it is hard to imagine anyone else having a shaping hand in his career. Doesn't the logo on every book, every comic, every film we've seen since childhood say **Walt Disney's Mickey Mouse**? Of course, when you stop to think of it, there must have been other artists over the years drawing those books and comics, and creating the thousands on thousands of celluloid paintings that brought Mickey to life on the screen. Yet it seems more fitting somehow to regard the mouse as Disney's personal handiwork.

That at least was the opinion of King Features, the syndicate that distributed the **Mickey** newspaper strip. Walt had originally credited Ub Iwerks, the animator who helped create Mickey and who penciled the first three weeks of dailies. If you are willing to dig through musty back files of newsprint, you will find Iwerks' byline in several papers—running, in some cases, for a good year after he left Disney's employ. Most papers, however, credited Walt Disney from the outset. Twenty years later, when the Studio was producing half a dozen strips, it occurred to Walt that it might be nice to let the cartoonists sign their own work. The syndicate was dismayed: introduce a lot of unknown names? That could only hurt the strips' market value. The public, they insisted, thought that Walt himself drew every panel—why shatter the illusion? So **Mickey** and the other titles remained in Disney's name.

Yet it was the Studio that finally allowed a collector named Malcolm Willits to meet and interview Floyd Gottfredson, the man who took over the **Mickey** strip in 1930 and was still drawing it in 1967. Once Willits' interview was

Mickey in 1938.

Mickey in 1988.

The Blot's elaborate deathtraps made him one of Mickey's most diabolical adversaries.

published, other fans sought out the artist. Gottfredson slowly acquired a following, a loyal core of fans, though not enough to make his name a household word. His first readers, now edging into their seventies, can hardly be expected to make a fuss about old comic strips; and a new generation has yet to discover him, for the Disney Company has done little to keep his work in print. Yet this artist is a force to be reckoned with: a relic of America's past and a major part of Mickey's history.

Let us introduce you.

ii

Floyd Gottfredson was born in a railway station in 1905 and raised in a one-horse town south of Salt Lake City. His family had shaken hands with poverty so often that the prospect no longer dismayed them; they simply grit their teeth and forged ahead, still regarding America as a land of promise. To earn money for art lessons, young Floyd went from door to door peddling copies of his grandfather's memoirs, vivid tales of Indian wars from a not-too-distant frontier era. While convalescing from a hunting accident, he read Horatio Alger stories and absorbed their bright, heroic, opportunistic ethic.

Following several minor cartooning jobs for Utah journals, he moved to Los Angeles, that gold coast of the entertainment industry. There, inspired one day by a glimpse of a **Mickey Mouse** movie poster, he took a job at the fledgling Disney Studio, signing on as an inbetweener, the entry-level position for animators. It was not quite what Gottfredson wanted—he had hoped to draw newspaper comics—but he developed a liking for the painstaking animation work. When Disney transferred him four months later to work on the new **Mickey** newspaper strip, his career really took off.

Gottfredson became second father to Disney's brainchild, the steward of Mickey's soul—at least in the comics. In 1929, of course, Disney was not giving the matter much thought. "All we ever intended for [Mickey] was that he should continue to make people everywhere chuckle with him and at him," he confessed years later. "We didn't burden him with any social symbolism; we made him no mouthpiece for frustration or harsh satire. Mickey was simply a little personality assigned to the purposes of laughter." In the earliest strips written by Disney, the mouse is little more than a mischief-maker raising cain around the barnyard. He twists a dachshund like a rubber band and ties a knot in a stork's neck, both typical cartoon gags. Gottfredson fell into step with more visual humor and even put Mickey on the receiving end of the rough antics. In one strip, Kat Nipp takes a pair of scissors to the mouse's tail!

Mickey gradually evolved beyond such low comedy. As the Studio's first success, he became an emblem for Walt of all that was right and good. From the outset Disney took a parental

Gottfredson felt that "everything was overwritten" in the early strips. "We finally came to learn that once you make a point, stop there for God's sake, and move on!"

interest in him, and this shaped Mickey's character. Animators soon learned that there were things Donald Duck might do—wild, farcical things—to which Mickey could not stoop. Where Donald was childish, Mickey was childlike. If Donald was devious, Mickey was open-hearted and honest. Donald expressed frustration; Mickey expressed joy. He was Walt's good icon and, thanks to the silver screen, the nation's as well.

Gottfredson's Mormon upbringing and his unflaggingly positive outlook made him the perfect keeper for this icon. Never complaining, choking back his hurts—this is how he dealt with poverty and the trauma of his accident, and this is the ethic he brought to Mickey. Gottfredson's mouse combines the virtues of good citizen and good soldier: he helps the underdog and fights for law and order. He is not above teasing Minnie and Clarabelle in a friendly way, and the comedic framework of the strip requires him to take an occasional pratfall; but his actions as a rule are selfless, courageous, and patriotic. With moral precepts and nuggets of right thinking, he also keeps our chins high and our feet on the straight and narrow.

"Whenever you have a job, no matter how hard it is, or how much you hate t' do it, just buckle down an' remember, th' mail must go through!" he tells Minnie at the triumphant conclusion of "The Mail Pilot."

If Mickey gains the upper hand in a battle, he remembers to be merciful, even to villains of the deepest dye. He is quick to reprove Horace Horsecollar when his friend suggests blowing up the mad scientists in "Blaggard Castle" along with their mansion: "They haven't really **hurt** anybody! . . . If everybody got punished for what he **wants** to do, the whole world would be living in jail!"

Is it any wonder Horace applauds: "Gosh Mickey. . . if everybody was like you, th' world wouldn't **need** t' be no better! It'd be good **enough!**"

Aside from a brief period in the late 1930s when Gottfredson had a bellyful of Mickey's virtuousness and hankered to create his own strip, he was behind the little mouse all the way. This sincerity in his storytelling enables the comic to transcend what today may seem like mawkish morality. Children have a remarkable ear for hypocrisy, far keener than ours: they can tell when adults are using Bucky Bug or Practical Pig to preach at them. Mickey may be upbeat, but he does not make a habit of dispensing moral sweetmeats. What's better, he combines his good cheer with guts, for he is encouraging not only himself but a whole nation. America desperately needed that encouragement in the wake of the Great Depression. We can use it no less today.

What draws us to the strip, however, is the entertainment it offers. Gottfredson was a deft storyteller who brought a wide range of subjects to his tales. Having worked several years as a projectionist, he had a good knowledge of films; he was also an aviation buff and an avid reader of mysteries. These interests provide both form and content for the **Mickey** serials. Boris Karloff's horror movies color the atmosphere of "Blaggard Castle"; "The Mail Pilot" reflects the popularity of comic strip aviators like Hal Forrest's **Tailspin Tommy**; and "The Phantom Blot" draws on the spy films and novels that became increasingly popular as America was catapulted toward World War II.

The Blot adventure is especially noteworthy for being one of several wartime tales in which the sharply-drawn values of Mickey's world begin to blur. The villain is no longer a familiar cutthroat like Peg-Leg Pete or Sylvester Shyster, but a man so totally masked that even his eyes appear blank. His intentions, like his person,

Most of Floyd Gottfredson's comic strip serials in 1932 and 1933 were adaptations of Disney cartoons. His story "The Great Orphanage Robbery," which took the rudimentary plot of "Mickey's Mellerdrammer" and turned it almost into a novel, ends with a long chase sequence in which Mickey follows the villainous **Peg-Leg Pete** and **Sylvester Shyster** to the Klondike—a setting inspired by another early cartoon, "The Klondike Kid."

seem unfathomable: he steals worthless cameras and leaves Mickey in elaborate deathtraps that always include an exit. Even when the Blot is captured and unmasked, we learn frustratingly little, only that he is the agent of a foreign power pursuing a doomsday weapon. Mickey for once has won no more than a skirmish.

Gottfredson worked on the strip for 45 years, retaining tight artistic control all the time. Inkers and dialog writers came and went, but Gottfredson roughed out each plot, drew the pencil art, and oversaw production—at least for six days of the week. The Sunday pages interested him less, and here he may have farmed out more of the basic chores. Certainly the dialog has a different tone, and the plotting is looser and lighter. These strips retain the cartoon influence far longer than the dailies: humor is often slapstick, characters burst into snatches of song, and bodies adjust in rubbery fashion to comic contortion, as when Mickey shortens a horse's tail by pulling at its neck or uses a plumber's helper to cure a dent in Uncle Amos' head. Even adventures like "Rumplewatt the Giant" and "Robin Hood" partake of this nonsensical flavor: they are bright visual romps rather than carefully plotted suspense tales. One suspects they were written with children in mind, boys and girls who would grab at the colorful Sunday comics but shy clear of the more adult cartoons buried in Dad's daily paper. Be that as it may, Gottfredson did not stint his artwork. The larger format seems to have given him new scope, and he rose to the challenge with some of his finest drawings.

iii

The America that Gottfredson knew is no longer part of our lives. From farmhouse to Senate house, we find our traditions crumbling, and our fictions reflect this upheaval. Comic strips have given way to comic books, comic books to television. Now television's audience is being eroded by widescreen blockbusters like "Raiders of the Lost Ark"—a film which Gottfredson felt had little point or substance. What will be next—participatory hologram videos? At one time nothing was more participatory than the act of reading.

Mickey Mouse, staunch trouper, has moved with the times. Since Disney took pains over the years to keep his child before the public, Mickey passed through many sets of creative hands, adapting as he went. When his animated shorts flagged in 1940, he became the Sorcerer's Apprentice in a pioneering film of Dukas' tone poem. When television invaded America's homes, he was flung onto the screen as host of a children's variety show. Five years ago, he made a comeback playing Bob Cratchit in an animated version of Dickens' **Christmas Carol**. Silhouetted on the Walt Disney World logo, he can even look high-tech and businesslike. But much of the old magic is gone.

Today the Mickey with which most of us are familiar is the large, plush doll that cavorts around the Disney parks and through ketchup commercials. He retains some of the childlike charm but none of the spunk of Gottfredson's mouse; yet children, seeing him on a travel poster, will squeal with happy recognition. As for the Mickey we find on greeting cards and other merchandise, he has adapted by acquiring a rumpled jacket, faded jeans, sneakers, and a digital watch. He looks like one of the heroes on **Miami Vice**—which is to say, a genial young lout.

If the Disney Company has seen fit to change Mickey's image this drastically, why do we look back to the old mouse? Partly because Gottfredson's strips offer such crackling good adventure yarns—that is the reason you bought this book and will open it time and again. But we like to think Gottfredson's Mickey will survive because he offers us a portrait of ourselves when young, a view of America's lost innocence. While other artists were using satire to explode contemporary forms and foibles, Gottfredson chose to cherish what he inherited. Rather than undermining the attitudes and fictions of the day, he worked within their bounds; instead of snarling at mankind's ills, he focused on the noble strain in our nature. This makes his comics perennially appealing.

Geoffrey Blum
September 20, 1988.

OF MOUSE AND THE MAN

Floyd Gottfredson and the Mickey Mouse Continuities

by Thomas Andrae

A small black mouse speeds through the sky in his monoplane. Six other pilots have disappeared—mysteriously, without a trace—but he is determined to get the mail through. The sky is clear, except for a lone black cloud. As he approaches, the cloud looms suddenly before him, moving strangely against the wind, the dark mass placing itself squarely in his path. Just as he is about to dive beneath, he sees something shocking: there, under the cloud, a hideous figure looms menacingly—a giant spider! He pummels the leering insect with a volley of machine-gun bullets to no effect. A giant web descends behind the bulbous black body and begins to attract the plane like a magnet, pulling it closer and closer...

To many, this scene from the 1933 comic strip adventure, "The Mail Pilot," may seem incongruous with the image we have inherited of Mickey Mouse. This is not the sweet, diffident mouse we are accustomed to. We forget that audiences growing up in the thirties—and into the fifties—knew two radically different Mickeys, the mouse of the animated cartoons and that of the newspaper comic strips. As comics historian Bill Blackbeard puts it, the comic strip Mickey was "a death-defying, tough, steel-gutted mouse quite unlike the mild, blandly benign mouse of contemporary Studio usage, who kept the kids of 1933 rapt with his adventures on pirate dirig-

ibles, cannibal islands, and bullet-tattered fighter planes."[1] Whereas the screen Mickey was famed for his romantic idylls and musical hijinx with Minnie, the comic strip mouse had little time for romance: he was involved in life-and-death struggles which could not be won through tricks of animation magic.

By the early thirties, Mickey had become an international star whose popularity rivaled that of Charlie Chaplin (one of the celebrities Walt Disney used to model the mouse). Children and adults flocked to watch his latest screen exploits, and intellectuals pondered his immense popularity, declaring Disney one of the great graphic artists of the twentieth century.

Mickey had some of his finest moments in the newspapers and his was virtually the only nationally syndicated strip which offered adult cliffhangers in the funny-animal genre. Animated cartoons, on the other hand, were

little more than strings of gags, held together by the barest semblance of a plot and brought abruptly to their climax by some concluding joke. Indeed, animation's focus on details of action and movement precluded any emphasis on plot and character, and dialog was virtually

---

[1] *Bill Blackbeard, "Mickey Mouse and the Phantom Artist," in The Comic Book Book, ed. Don Thompson and Dick Lupoff (New Rochelle, NY: Arlington House, 1973), p. 38.*

MICKEY'S MAGIC LAMP

"Mickey's Magic Lamp"—changed to "Pluto's Dream House" (*Pluto* cartoon Prod. 2240, released August 30, 1940)—inspired a one-page featurette in *Good Housekeeping Magazine* (left), and was the springboard for Gottfredson's *Mickey Mouse* serial, "The Miracle Master" (above left).

non-existent. Comic strip adventures offered an alternative to these skeletal stories. Serialized over three or four months, they were allowed time to build complex plots and rounded characters.

Though Disney supervised all his cartoon shorts, they were still group efforts, passing through many sets of hands and becoming diluted in the process. The **Mickey** strips, though still produced by a team, were primarily the work of one man who at various times was responsible for plotting, drawing, and inking. As a result, a single personal vision emerged. This one man was the main **Mickey Mouse** artist to draw the strip for over forty-five years, until he retired in the mid-seventies. In the late 1960s, dilligent fans sought him out, and he began at last to receive the acclaim he deserved. The man's name was Floyd Gottfredson.

Rude Beginnings

Like the strip he drew, Gottfredson's biography reads like a piece of Americana: "I was born May 5, 1905," he recalled, "in, believe it or not, a railway station in Kaysville, Utah. I was raised in a small town, Siggurd, one hundred eighty miles south of Salt Lake City."[2] The future mouse-artist's interest in drawing was sparked by an accident he suffered at the age of eleven. His mother had sent him to church on Sunday, but Floyd and a cousin decided to go hunting instead. Young Gottfredson had been taught never to point a gun, so he carried the rifle with the barrel turned inward. As he handed it to his cousin, the gun was thought to have caught

on a twig, and Floyd shot himself badly in the arm.

This accident changed his whole life. No longer could he play outside with other children; he had to stay home, recuperating from nine operations to repair the damaged limb. To have some indoor activity, he developed an interest in art, which bloomed under his mother's encouragement. Gottfredson's sister, Mrs. Jessie Furby, fondly recalls that one of Floyd's first drawings was a portrait of his mother, made while sitting at her knee.[3] Since there were no art schools in the vicinity, he began taking drawing instructions by correspondence.

Gottfredson's father opposed this budding art career, feeling that his son should get a job like other boys. But the injury to Gottfredson's hand would not allow him to hold a regular job. Like other great artists who have turned tragedy to advantage, he persisted, and, drawing with his bad hand, he eventually developed a drawing style that compensated for his physical limita-

King Features Syndicate wanted Gottfredson to redo this alligator-pit cliff-hanger, complaining that "women were so squeamish" about such things. Walt refused.

tions. Because he had lost most of the flexibility in his hand, he had to draw by moving his entire arm—something that is taught in penmanship classes, but which artists are rarely trained to do. This gave his drawings a sweep and flair few others attain.

During his convalescence, Gottfredson read a small stack of Horatio Alger books. "I belonged to an organization called the Lone Scouts. They had a national magazine, and my uncle wrote to them and told them about my accident and asked other kids to write to me.

---

[2] *Series of interviews with Floyd Gottfredson, September 27 and December 12, 1979 and February 26, 1981.*

[3] *Mrs. Furby recalls that "when Floyd's arm was shot, the doctors decided to amputate. My dear mother said, 'No,' and wouldn't permit it. That's when they tried nine operations and saved it as best they could in those 'horse and buggy' days. [Do you] call it a Mother's Faith? Or Providence? I prefer to think yes to both!" From a letter to the publisher, April 19, 1988.*

Gottfredson's first *Mickey* strip was an almost slavish duplication of Win Smith's rendering and characterization of the mouse.

Walt Disney drew this 1926 birthday card for his father, populating it with mice that prefigure Mickey. Final design of the Mouse in 1928 was by animator Ub Iwerks.

Kids from all over the country sent me letters and things, including forty-two Horatio Alger books. After that I gravitated to boys' adventure books and detective stories."[4] This diet of pulp and punch provided raw material for the character of Mickey for future adventures: the mouse would become another Horatio Alger hero, struggling to overcome his lack of size, strength, and advantage.

Gottfredson's first professional job was that of projectionist and advertising artist for a small movie theater chain. In 1926 he began taking another correspondence course, with the Federal Schools of Illustrating and Cartooning. In 1928, at the suggestion of Federal, he entered a national cartoon contest and placed second. On the strength of this showing, he quit his job as projectionist and moved his family to Los Angeles, hoping to find work as a newspaper cartoonist. But he could not find a position with any of the papers and was forced to resume his former occupation.

His decision to apply at the Disney Studio was the result of a chance encounter that had all the marks of destiny. "Late in 1929, the theater I was working in was torn down to extend the street through the site, and I was out of work. I was looking on what was then known as 'film row' [Vermont Avenue], where all the film exchanges were located, when I saw a one-sheet movie poster of Mickey Mouse in front of the exchange that distributed Walt Disney's films. Out of curiosity, I went in, and the fellow there told me about Walt creating Mickey after losing Oswald to his distributor. He said that Walt was going to New York the next week to hire artists. I rushed home to get my portfolio, went to the Studio, and got the job that afternoon."[5]

When Gottfredson expressed interest in becoming a newspaper cartoonist, Disney talked him out of the idea. King Features Syndicate had asked for a **Mickey Mouse** comic strip, and Disney already had artists at work on it. So he hired Gottfredson as an **inbetweener**, the entry-

level position for would-be animators. Perhaps as a concession, however, he did make Gottfredson backup man on the strip.

Perhaps because Disney had always wanted to be a comic strip artist himself, he wrote **Mickey Mouse** in its early months. Ub Iwerks, who did the final design of Mickey's appearance and almost singlehandedly animated the first **Mickey** cartoons, did the drawing. Another artist, Win Smith, inked Iwerks' pencils. When Iwerks quit Disney's to open his own cartoon studio, Smith took over the pencil work as well. "But four months after the strip started, Win had a blowup with Walt," Gottfredson recalled. "Walt was trying to get him to take over the writing because he didn't have time for it anymore. Because of Walt's prodding, Smith quit; and since Walt hired me as backup man on the strip, he asked me to take it over. By now I had

become very interested in animation and told Walt I'd rather stay in it. So Walt asked me to take over the strip for two weeks until he could find another artist to do it. Nothing further was ever said about it, and I continued to draw the **Mickey** daily for forty-five-and-a-half years—until my retirement in October 1975."[6]

The first strips had loose continuity; they were gag-a-day sequences adapted from early **Mickey** cartoons. The initial week's sequence, based on the first produced **Mickey** short, "Plane Crazy," reflected Disney's rural origins. It was set in a barnyard and shows the mouse in a hayloft dreaming of becoming an aviator

---

[4] *Gottfredson interviews.*

[5] Ibid.

[6] Ibid.

like his hero Lindbergh.[7] The humor was based on animation-styled gags with Mickey using a dachshund like a rubber band to power his plane and a turkey's feathers as a tail fin. The 1931 cartoon, "The Castaway," in production at the time, provided a plot beginning during the second week: Mickey finds himself marooned on a jungle island. A high point of the cartoon is the scene where Mickey tricks an alligator into swallowing a lion that is chasing him, then uses the lion's tail to tie the gator's jaws shut. In the comic strip, however, the gag is stilted, broken into three static panels and lacking the fast, zany pacing of the animation. Clearly, the strip needed new focus—but in what direction?

The nudge came from King Features, who had observed the growing popularity of radio serials

---

[7] *Charles A. Lindbergh, an American aviator, became a national hero in 1927, piloting his* Spirit of St. Louis *in the world's first non-stop solo flight across the Atlantic.*

In this early cartoon, a mad scientist attempts a bizarre experiment on Pluto, until Mickey comes to his pet's rescue. In the end, the entire episode turns out to have been Mickey's nightmare. In "Blaggard Castle"—inspired by "The Mad Doctor"—the menace was more realistic and more frightening.

like **Amos 'n' Andy.** Serialized strips like Sidney Smith's **The Gumps** and Roy Crane's **Wash Tubbs** were fast replacing gag-a-day comics, and in March 1930, the syndicate asked Disney to turn **Mickey Mouse** into a continuity. Disney complied, and the first adventure story, "Mickey Mouse in Death Valley," began on March 31. Gottfredson assumed the art chores in April, with his first strip being published on May 5. Disney continued doing the writing for two more weeks. Then Gottfredson took over as both artist and writer until late 1932. After that, as manager of the comic strip department, he began to bring in other writers and inkers. Though the strip was no longer a solo effort, Gottfredson continued to plot each continuity and draw the pencil art, setting both the story-line and visual style.[8]

The first segment of "Mickey Mouse in Death Valley" is based on a 1929 cartoon called "The Haunted House," in which Mickey has a tryst with a ghost. Needing greater mystery to build suspense and provide a framework for the strip's plot, Disney had replaced the ghost with a black-clad figure called the Fox. Despite the haunted house motif, the real threat in this story is economic, not gothic.

The villains are Peg-Leg Pete—an oversized alley cat with a wooden leg who serves as Mickey's chief nemesis in the cartoons—and Sylvester Shyster, a top-hatted rat that Disney created for the strip. Shyster, as his name implies, is a crooked lawyer with designs on Minnie's inheritance, which includes a secret gold mine. The plot derives, of course, from the melodramatic clichés of silent cinema which

Widely circulated news reports of a record-setting $63,800 sale in a June 8, 1988, New York auction of an animated celluloid from the 1933 Disney classic, "The Mad Doctor," failed to note that the overlay was not used in the film, though the background was original. The figure and "skeleton stairs" cel was created in 1934—in black and white, as was the cartoon—as an illustration for page 59 of *Mickey Mouse's Movie Stories Book 2*, published by the David McKay Co. (Photo courtesy of Christie's East/Private Collector Canada.)

were so popular in the years prior to the **Mickey** strip. Mickey is the stalwart youth who rescues his kidnaped sweetheart, then saves her fortune by recovering a stolen map.

The threat posed by Shyster and Pete seems particularly apt when we consider that the story appeared only months after the great stock market crash of 1929. Villains in the early melodramas had often represented oppressive economic forces, taking the form of heartless landlords and scheming swindlers. These stereotyped figures offered audiences a way of negotiating the tensions caused by America's

transition from a self-sufficient agrarian culture to an industrial society governed by the pursuit of profit. The shyster figure, however, had an immediate appeal to audiences in the thirties. At the nadir of the Depression (1930-1933), many films were made featuring corrupt lawyers, crooked politicians, and sleazy newspapermen.[9]

---

[8] *For a list of other artists and writers on the* Mickey *strip and the dates of their work, see pp. 185–192.*

[9] *Andrew Bergman,* We're in the Money: Depression America and Its Films *(New York: Harper and Row, 1971), p. 18.*

14

"Floyd and Madge," ca. 1910, picturing a four- or five-year-old Gottfredson; and, lower right, Gottfredson as an adolescent before his crippling shotgun accident.

Floyd Gottfredson in 1931, about a year after he had begun to draw *Mickey Mouse*.

The shyster also appeared as a fast-talking city con man—an embodiment of the great moral weaknesses people feared in urban life. In American folklore, rural America (and later, the small town) was enshrined as an Arcadian Eden, free of the corruption of the urban metropolis. The shyster thus seemed to embody all that was wrong with the country, offering a tangible, easily understood threat. But as Andrew Bergman points out, it was not the hand in the till but the emptiness of the till that was the problem. The films' blaming the shyster suggested that it was not failed institutions but con men that were the problem and getting rid of crooks was the answer, not overhauling the economy. Thus, ironically, blaming such scapegoats only reinforced the institutions which had brought the country to its crisis.

Gottfredson's next story, the first he wrote entirely by himself, also involves an economic threat. "Mr. Slicker and the Egg Robbers" makes explicit the urban nature of the menace that was implicit in Sylvester Shyster. Slicker is a con artist who turns Minnie's head with his city ways at the same time that he steals her father's

eggs and threatens him with bankruptcy.

Again the melodramatic and the Depression's concerns dovetail and the shyster is blamed for the economic crisis. To ensure that Minnie will marry him, Slicker robs the local bank, throwing the entire community into destitution—an event which mirrors the bank failures of the time. Mickey's exposure of Slicker both saves Minnie from the proverbial Fate Worse Than Death and restores economic security, offering a happy ending for Depression readers.

"Slicker" is a transitional story that moves from the barnyard and what Horst Schroeder calls the "rustic anarchy" of the strip's first weeks[10] to the small-town no-man's land in which Mickey would reside for the rest of the decade. The small-town setting provided a community in which more sophisticated adventures could take place. In "Slicker," Gottfredson introduced two themes that would characterize some of his best later stories: the sensational crime and the mysterious master criminal whose activities force Mickey to play amateur detective.

At the same time, the story shows Gottfredson experimenting. "Death Valley" had been a mixture of horror story and western; this time, the artist mixed two other genres, the romance and the crime drama. Nor had he yet perfected the difficult blend of humor and sustained sus-

pense required by an adventure serial. Gags in both stories are often gratuitous, interrupting the narrative rather than moving it forward. And the villains are poorly defined, lacking the combination of mystery and sinister menace that would characterize his later criminal masterminds.

Adapting the Cartoons

In effect, Gottfredson was serving his apprenticeship during these two years. For him to do a "serious" funny-animal adventure, it required two things that are also needed in real-life adventure strips. First, Gottfredson had to master the serial format. Each strip had to end on a puzzle or cliff-hanger that would make readers turn to the next day's strip. The opening panel had to summarize the immediately preceding action, so that readers who missed a day or two could still follow the story; and the entire strip had to advance the general plot. Not easy.

Second—and in the funny-animal genre, this could be credited as his invention—Gottfredson had to make Mickey's perils realistic and threatening enough to create suspense, yet keep them tongue-in-cheek. Humor could not rely too heavily on slapstick, nor on the physically out-

[10] *Horst Schroeder, Introduction to* Walt Disney's Goofy *(New York: Abbeville Press, 1979), p. 13.*

landish events that propelled the cartoons, because this would disturb the suspension of disbelief necessary to carry an adventure story.

The blend that Gottfredson sought had rarely been achieved in comics before, even among the realistic humor strips. Fortunately, the **Mickey** cartoons themselves began to change in the early thirties, in ways that made them adaptable as newspaper continuities. Peter Adamakos has pointed to the disparity in styles between the first **Mickey** cartoons and those that followed, a difference he attributes to the fact that Disney himself was involved in making the first three cartoons, but left the next few in the care of Ub Iwerks, while he dealt with commercial matters. Then, starting in 1931, according to Adamakos, there was a marked improvement in the quality of Disney's output. His cartoons were no longer just collections of gags that carried on until it was time to end, but finely crafted narratives. These advances Adamakos attributes to Iwerks' departure from the Studio.[11]

This assessment, however, is one-sided. The transition from fantasy-based Mickey cartoons to more coherent stories involved losses as well as gains. The early shorts operate in a magical universe: a surreal world where there is no fixed order and objects are plastic to imagination and will. Film critic Robert Sklar has pointed out that, as Disney's cartoons became more coherent narratives, they lost the untrammeled fantasy of their predecessors and turned moralistic. The **Mickey** shorts became conventional melodramas with heroes, villains, and happy endings.[12] Yet Sklar is wrong to assume that fantasy elements were dropped; instead they were modified to make them more plausible. So the shorts provided the much-needed model for Gottfredson's blend of adventure and fantasy. In fact, they inspired him to create a series of comic strip adaptations. These stories reveal qualities of characterization and pacing that anticipate Gottfredson's best work.

From 1932 to 1933, most of Gottfredson's

serials were adaptations of cartoons, beginning on January 11, 1932, with his reworking of "Mickey's Mellerdrammer." A comparison between cartoon and strip—"The Great Orphanage Robbery"— shows how much Gottfredson developed the still rudimentary plot into an almost novelistic treatment. The cartoon is concerned only with Mickey's attempt to stage **Uncle Tom's Cabin** with the help of his friends.

"Walt asked me to take a couple of the mice in the audience in 'Orphan's Benefit,'" Gottfredson recalled, "and make nephews out of them for Mickey." They were to wear skirts and sailor hats and have a "little spiked tail sticking up so that the skirt could drape over it," which Frank Reilly never liked. "I had to keep reminding him that this was Walt's innovation, and his idea."

Gottfredson's version adds motivation: the play is produced as a benefit to raise money for an orphans' home. Better, it turns the entire scenario into a crime thriller by having Pete and Shyster steal the orphanage money, inaugurating a long chase sequence in which Mickey follows them to the Klondike—a setting inspired by another early cartoon, "The Klondike Kid."

Gottfredson's mastery of the serial format is evident in nearly every strip of this adventure. First we are enticed into the story by following Mickey's attempt each day to increase the running total for the orphans' fund. Then the sus-

pense increases through the use of cross-cutting techniques derived from old movie serials: the strip cuts back and forth between the trial, conviction, and near-lynching of Horace Horsecollar, who is falsely accused of the theft, and Mickey's progress in tracking down the villains. Gottfredson's graphics also contribute to the story's drama: he evoked a sense of breathless excitement by drawing pronounced beads of sweat popping from each character's face, a trademark of his style that he borrowed from Iwerks' early strips and the animated cartoons.[13]

The Depression had shaken some of America's oldest and most cherished beliefs, especially that of the self-made man in which an individual's temperance and hard work would surely bring success and prosperity. In feature films, cartoons, and comic strips of the period, popular artists again attempted to reassert and make credible this old cultural idea. Thus in "The Great Orphanage Robbery" Gottfredson imbued Mickey with a Horatio Alger ethos. Like Alger's Ragged Dick, Mickey is a youngster able to succeed through hard work, ingenuity, and a happy arrangement of circumstances—pluck and luck, as Alger would have it.[14] When Mickey saves a man's life, the man

---

[11] *Peter Adamakos, "Ub Iwerks," Mindrot, No. 7 (June 15, 1977), pp. 20–24.*

[12] *Robert Sklar, Movie-Made America: A Cultural History of American Movies (New York: Vintage Books, 1975), pp. 200–205.*

[13] *The "beads of sweat" were probably not intended to convey that precise image, but were a symbol of expressed emotion or emphasized reaction. . . like an exclamation point. Gottfredson drew them throughout his career, but used the beads more selectively as his art matured.*

[14] *Folklore has distorted the Alger hero: John Cawelti points out that the Alger boy does not achieve success solely through his own powers but is aided by good connections and fortuitous coincidences; and he achieves only a modest financial and occupational position, rather than rising from rags to riches. See John Cawelti, Apostles of the Self-Made Man: Changing Concepts of Success in America (Chicago: University of Chicago Press, 1965), p. 109.*

turns out to be a millionaire who offers to double all the money our hero earns. And when he wishes he could win a glider race, a gust of wind miraculously transforms his advertising sandwich boards into a high-flying glider, and he wins first place in the contest.

The fact that the success of Gottfredson's Mickey depends on such coincidences and miracles reveals how great the perceived gap was between success and individual effort during the Depression. Indeed, the hard work Mickey performs is not even connected with his reward, except in terms of making him deserving. Instead, his wishes are fulfilled by chance, in a manner reminiscent of the Alger stories and **Cinderella**. This magiclike quality allows him to function as a utopian symbol, a promise of happiness and fulfillment in a better future. Leaping fire hydrants as he expounds his dreams, or happily sailing through the air with his makeshift wings, Gottfredson's mouse is a character of great cheerfulness and vitality, a source of joy and hope in a troubled world.

Perhaps "Blaggard Castle" (reprinted in this volume), which was inspired by the 1933 cartoon "The Mad Doctor," is Gottfredson's finest adaptation. In the cartoon, a mad scientist attempts a bizarre experiment on Pluto and a chicken, until Mickey comes to his pet's rescue. In the end, the entire episode turns out to have been Mickey's nightmare. In "Blaggard Castle," however, the menace is more realistic and much more frightening: a hypnotic ray turns Horace into a mindless slave and potential killer, so that Mickey is attacked by his best friend. Using this ray, a trio of evil scientists plans to enslave the world by hypnotizing people to murder at will and to bring them "food and jewels and gold." Gottfredson augmented the gothic atmosphere of his strip by modeling his scientists on Boris Karloff from a movie he had just seen. He gave them the dark, deep-set eyes of the homicidal butler played by Karloff in **The Old Dark House** (1932).

Gottfredson's use of science-fiction technology also added to the story's other-worldly, gothic feel. In the early 1930s, the idea of any type of closed-circuit television—much less a televiewer like the one used by Professors Ecks and Doublex, which had the capacity to tune in, view, and listen to anyone, anywhere—seemed beyond possibility to most people. Norman Gottfredson recalls seeing the **Mickey** strips on his father's drawing board and telling him that such an invention was too far out to be believed. The elder Gottfredson was concerned that the devices in his comics be as plausible as possible, so he researched the subject to prove closed-circuit TV could and did exist. He later took his son to see a working model.[15]

So effective was the gothic atmosphere in "Blaggard Castle," it brought about Gottfredson's first brush with censorship. "Two mad scientists got hold of Mickey in their dungeon and lowered him into an alligator pit. The only escape route was across a pit of hungry alligators to a ledge on the other side. Mickey found a feeding stick and vaulted across. He got halfway across, and the pole broke. We left him suspended there. The syndicate sent us a frantic wire saying that we had to cut out this entire alligator sequence because reptiles shocked women and children and were offensive. There was no way we could do it over and get it to the papers in time. So I took the photostats to Walt, and he said, 'To hell with them! You forget it, and I'll either call them or wire them and tell them to go to hell.' So the sequence was left in; in cases like this he was more powerful than they were."[16]

In "The Mad Doctor," Mickey escapes from the scientist and awakens from his dream. In Gottfredson's tale, he turns the hypnotic ray on the villains and transforms them into servants of humanity. The contrast between those who use science for selfish ends and those who use it for the common good had a special meaning for Depression audiences. It represented a shift from the laissez-faire ethic of the robber barons and their age, to the charity of Franklin D. Roosevelt's welfare state. Roosevelt's New Deal signaled an end to nineteenth-century individualism and placed a new emphasis on social security, government regulation, and collective action.

At this time, America was plagued by riots, looting, strikes, and even pitched battles with police—mostly in industrial areas and in larger cities. There were, among those in the country who were the nearest to these unhappy events, officials who feared that a swelling revolutionary fervor could lead to a possible attempt by the masses to overthrow the government by force and to seize power! Films like **King Kong**, with its climactic scene in which Kong bursts his chains and goes on a destructive rampage through New York, symbolized what audiences most feared (and perhaps secretly enjoyed): the liberation of lawless, primitive, and bestial forces that were presumed to lie dormant within the collective unconscious. So the comic strip image of the scientist as a power-mad tyrant who could transform the masses into a murderous mob who would seize the country's resources, was deeply meaningful.

"The Mail Pilot," a 1933 **Mickey** short, inspired another classic Gottfredson adaptation (reprinted in this volume). Both cartoon and strip deal with Mickey's duty to deliver the mail,

---

[15] *The first actual working model of electrically scanned television dates back to 1922. Gottfredson's research verified press reports he had undoubtedly read.*

[16] *Gottfredson interviews.*

and his battle with Peg-Leg Pete, who turns up this time as an air pirate. But here the similarities end, for Gottfredson expanded his plot into a pulp epic. The cartoon film focuses on minute details—often physically impossible action—as vehicles for comedy. Mickey wears windshield wipers on his goggles; and his airplane is anthropomorphized, so that it wiggles its tail and says "ouch" when hit by lightning.

Such ingenious impossibilities are funny in an animated cartoon and are part of the fantasy, but would be out of place in a more serious adventure tale. Gottfredson's story emphasizes instead Mickey's learning experiences: he is not a pilot at the outset, as in the cartoon, but must study and practice to earn his wings. The mouse's initial blunders allow for comedy at the same time that they build his character as an Alger hero who must work dilligently to achieve his goal.

When the cartoon opens, Pete is already known to be the villain behind a series of airplane robberies; we see his wanted poster on a wall. The main excitement derives from Mickey's dogfight with Pete and his triumphant return to the base with the villain neatly trussed. Gottfredson transformed this simple bring-'em-back-alive plot into a mystery thriller by having the planes disappear without a trace; the element of robbery is secondary in his story. A giant "spider" augments this aura of mystery with gothic horror. And Pete himself is a far more sinister figure in the strip. Like the seafaring pirates of old who made their victims walk the plank, he and Shyster force Mickey to walk off the platform of their dirigible to what they assume is his doom. Pete and Shyster's crimes are also more grandiose than those Pete commits in the cartoon. The two evil partners have built an entire city from their plunder. In fact, Plunderville contains some of Gottfredson's most biting parody, playing on the incongruity between the villains' illegal activities and respectable civic organizations. Over the entrance to the city hangs a sign that reads, "Patronize Home Industry;" another placcard announces, "Rotary Club Meets Tuesdays." The idea of a secret citadel built from stolen goods—hovering unsuspected above America's cities and looting at will—plays once again on the fear and delight that Depression audiences took in the image of the power-mad tyrant. Plunderville also offers the interesting ideological inversion of a proletarian brigand as tyrant, rather than the industrialists and stock market speculators who were universally blamed for the country's misfortunes.

Sometimes a real person, if colorful enough, could spark a continuity. One of Mickey's greatest foes, the Bat Bandit, was inspired by Gottfredson's reading about the Mexican revolutionary leader and long-time outlaw Pancho Villa. The artist's interest in Villa may have stemmed from the disappearance of his uncle, famed western silent film star Art Accord, into the wilds of Mexico. **Viva Villa**, a movie about the bandit starring Wallace Beery, was released just prior to Gottfredson's serial and may also have been an inspiration.

There are parallels between Don Jollio (the man beneath the bat mask) and Villa: both are Mexican bandits with long, curved mustaches, and both are cattle rustlers. Don Jollio, always smiling, is completely evil—like the villains in most westerns—and turns out not even to be Mexican, but an American crook in disguise, faking his accent.

"The Bat Bandit of Inferno Gulch" shows Gottfredson's mastery at last of the "funny animal" adventure, a genre described by Donald Duck/Uncle Scrooge artist Carl Barks as "characters in serious perils while at the same time they solve their problems by humorous means."[17] The climactic fight between Mickey and the bandit especially reveals Gottfredson's grasp of this principle. The life-and-death struggle is realistic and threatening: Mickey is thrown over a cliff. But he rebounds off a branch, grabs Don Don Jollio's serape, and spins him like a top off the edge, so that the bandit is left hanging by the tips of his boots: a comic resolution to the fight. Gags like this derive from cartoon slapstick, where characters are spun, flattened, and stretched for humorous effect; but the comic strip artist must handle them in a nuanced way, so that an action **appears** plausible, concealing its physical impossibility. In cartoons, on the other hand, humor is everything, and an action often becomes funny **because** we know it cannot happen. "The Bat Bandit" shows Gottfredson moving on from cartoon adaptations, creating his own villain, his own story, and about to embark on some of his best work.

The Mouse Grows Up

In the early thirties, Mickey was reckless,

---

[17] *Interview with Carl Barks by Donald Ault and Thomas Andrae, August 4, 1975.*

"The Bat Bandit of Inferno Gulch" was another of Gottfredson's masterful, black-clad, shadowy villains—a stateside outlaw posing as a Mexican rancher.

happy-go-lucky, mischievous, fallible, and liable to strong emotions.

By the middle of the decade Mickey had assumed a new role, becoming more serious and responsible. In films like "Mickey's Circus" and "The Band Concert," he became a little leader, organizing and managing the activities of others. This meant that he had to become a straight man, while his bumbling helpers got the laughs. Deprived of the comic foibles that made the other characters interesting, he became less interesting and began to be upstaged by Donald, Goofy, and even Pluto. He was far too idealized by this time to be allowed to do anything naughty or irresponsible.

"Mickey's our problem child," Disney admitted in the early fifties. "He's so much of an institution that we're limited in what we can do with him.... Mickey must always be sweet and lovable. What can you do with such a leading man?"[18]

The mouse was growing up. Hitherto, he had been portrayed in both films and comics as a youth who had to prove himself in a world of adults, battling large, powerful characters like Pete and Shyster. Now Mickey **himself** was an adult. Because Gottfredson always tried to follow the look and personality of the cartoon mouse, by the mid-thirties his Mickey was changed to become a cool-headed, efficient problem-solver who was almost always in control. His appearance also reflected a new maturity. He would continue to wear the famous red two-button shorts until the early forties, but his pipe-stem arms and legs grew thicker, and his oversize brogans, which once made him look like a boy trying to fill a man's shoes, shrank to accommodate the proportions of his body.

Mickey's new maturity is evident in "Editor-in-Grief," in which the mouse is owner and editor of a daily paper, with Donald and Goofy as his bungling employees. No longer concerned just with fulfilling his own ambitions or helping a personal friend, Mickey displays a sense of civic responsibility: he is a crusading journalist, refusing to be intimidated in his battle against graft and corruption. He exposes the collusion between Pete and Councilman Catfur, and even unmasks Police Commissioner Hogg (whose name suggests the grafter's greed). He is fully in charge at all times, and comedy is left to Donald and Goofy.

This serial was inspired by gangster films of the early thirties, like James Cagney's **Public Enemy** and Edward G. Robinson's **Little Caesar**. The protagonists of such films were often immensely popular, for they possessed a vitality that made the upholders of law and order seem insipid by comparison. Like the Alger hero, the gangster became a success through hard work and determination; but he operated outside the law and had to be killed in the last reel. In the mid-thirties, however, the media made a conscious effort to create a benevolent image of the federal government, and especially of the new F.B.I. Actors like Cagney and Robinson, who had earlier played gangsters, now became G-men. And in Gottfredson's strip, the gangster is aptly portrayed by the dyed-in-the-wool villain Peg-Leg Pete.

As we have seen, the notion of the shyster city, the immoral urban milieu, provided a popular explanation for the country's ills during the Depression. In "Editor-in-Grief," however, the image takes on a new function. It is not the individual chiseling of Sylvester Shyster ("Death Valley") or the contamination of rural life by one bad egg ("Mr. Slicker"). Instead, corruption has become an epidemic, infecting high officials and threatening the very fabric of society. Andrew Bergman suggests that Americans have always been intrigued as well as repulsed by corruption,[19] and Gottfredson's story reflects a fascination with the real-life gangsterism that ruled during the Prohibition era. As in the shyster stories, all the conflicts are resolved by bringing the villains to justice—a peremptory form of closure that never looks beneath the status quo to question social or economic institutions.

Mickey again takes the part of leader and Donald and Goofy the roles of his hapless helpers in the 1936 adventure "The Seven Ghosts." The story derives only vaguely from the Disney cartoon "Lonesome Ghosts," in which the spooks are real and lure the would-be ghost-busters to an old mansion to play pranks on them. In Gottfredson's tale, on the other hand, the ghosts are really smugglers in disguise using the mansion as a hideout. The story was inspired by films like **The Old Dark House** and the silent classic **The Cat and the Canary**. In the latter, a murderer uses secret passageways

---

[18] *Quoted in Richard Holliss and Brian Sibley,* Walt Disney's Mickey Mouse: His Life and Times *(New York: Harper and Row, 1986), p. 69.*

[19] *Bergman, p. 18.*

In "Editor-in-Grief," Gottfredson incorporated the classic gangster movie scene of a black limousine speeding by and discharging a hail of machine-gun bullets.

in an old mansion to menace a group of guests, just as the smugglers do in Gottfredson's strip.

"The Seven Ghosts" brings together all the elements that characterize Gottfredson's best work. Mickey is not the inept ghostbuster of "Lonesome Ghosts" but again the clear-headed problem-solver. But throughout much of the story neither he nor the reader can be certain whether the ghosts haunting Colonel Basset's mansion are real or not, and this element of doubt makes it one of Gottfredson's more intriguing mysteries. Like Mickey, the reader must sift through clues and contradictory evidence. Not until the end of the story, when the ghosts leave their footprints in spilled flour, can we be reasonably certain that they are not spirits.

Mickey, as leader of the detectives, is very much the Holmesian reasoner, fitting together scraps of evidence to reveal that the seven haunts are really smugglers. Here Gottfredson took pains to explain each ghostly trick—phosphorescent paint, hidden passages, etc.—so that the reader can be privy to every secret. His insistence on explaining away supernatural events would continue throughout the years of his involvement with the strip, strengthening Mickey's role as a level-headed adult and imparting a highly rationalistic ethos to the comic. It was a conviction that the spectral and the magical can usually be accounted for scientifically.

The story can be read as an allegory of the times. By 1936, the worst economic trials seemed to be over; but in fact the Depression lingered and was not fully overcome until World War II's economic boom. During these harrowing times, the country appeared to be in a slough from which there was no escape. Yet the Depression was so confusing and debilitating, one of the reactions to it was denial. People flocked to movie musicals which oozed glamor, luxury and good times, gangster films which showed that the success ethic still worked (albeit only outside the law), and listened by the millions to radio comedians who turned everything into a joke. This need for escapism is reflected in the opening of Gottfredson's story in which the townspeople deny the spirits' existence but are so frightened by them that even the word **ghost** throws them into a panic. The police, like officials in the Depression, are at a loss what to do, though they try to convince the public that everything is under control.

Gottfredson evoked the Depression explicitly when a ghost explains to Mickey that they have decided to haunt the Basset mansion because "the unemployment situation is terrible!" In effect, the ghosts are freebooters, sponging off the wealthy and thus evoking the fears, prevalent among officials at the time, that welfare relief might become an enervating sinecure.

At the center of these events is Colonel Basset, another Depression stereotype and the object of Gottfredson's satire of the upper

classes—a favorite theme in his later works. An eccentric who perpetually wears formal dress, but dons boxing gloves to keep from biting his nails, the colonel is so concerned with maintaining an aristocratic facade he is unable to cope with crises in his own house. He is more concerned with his inability to keep servants than his wife's terrified departure when the mansion becomes haunted. He even acts as his own butler to maintain appearances. His rage at the ghosts is not so much for their invasion of Basset manor, as for their not being gentlemen. Rather than helping to solve the mystery, he gets in Mickey's way. He represents the idle rich who, having lost everything in the stock market crash, go to absurd lengths to keep up the pretense that they still enjoy wealth and status, and who are ineffectual in coming to terms with—let alone solving—the problems of the times.

Mickey's assistants are equally ineffectual: Donald is too terrified and Goofy too dim-witted to be of much help. The law is also useless, the police sergeant paralyzed with fear, but also arrogant and self-serving . . . more interested in taking credit for a case he did not solve than in actually bringing the crooks to justice. Besides Mickey, only the smugglers are clever and resourceful, but their abilities are perverted in the service of crime. So Mickey alone has the will, intelligence, and moral fiber to act effectively and rightly.

This is, of course, the standard myth of the hero, the man who can single-handedly restore order to a chaos-riven society. In later stories, Gottfredson's world view would grow more complex. Although Mickey would usually triumph, in some cases he could fail disastrously, ironically becoming a victim of his own good deeds. In other stories, though he might defeat the villain, Mickey was forced to use questionable means. In short, Gottfredson would soon lose his rose-colored glasses as, indeed, America was losing its innocence.

This shift in Gottfredson's—as in America's—outlook is manifest in other ways as well. In the early stories, Mickey was a private citizen, struggling with personal enemies and helping personal friends. In the mid-thirties, he explicitly becomes an agent of the social order, often working for the U.S. Secret Service or serving as an honorary member of the police force. Increasingly, his battles are displaced onto foreign menaces in distant lands. America, once staunchly isolationist, was at last responding to the threat of totalitaranism in Europe. Foreign worries began to replace domestic ones, with the economic problems on the home front being buried in the urgency of the international situation. As historian Richard Pells writes, "By the mid-thirties, having created the Third Reich in his own special image, Adolf Hitler was ready (with the help of Italy and Japan) to remodel the world. Thus the crisis in Europe and the Far East supplanted the depression as the decade's

In the "The Pirate Submarine," Mickey is a Secret Service agent who battles Dr. Vulter, a would-be foreign dictator who captures men and ships at sea as the first step in his scheme for world domination. The analogy to Naziism is clear: Vulter wears a monocle and fancy dress uniform like the typical military tyrant, but he is a gorilla, and a ferocious-looking one at that, suggesting a bestial, sub-human nature. Vulter preys on the shipping lanes with a submarine, and its evil nature is manifest in the sharklike grin painted on its bow, and the wicked-looking eyes on its turret. Mickey fights back with his "submarplane," a combination of submarine and airplane. Not only does Gottfredson's invention of this vessel show once more his love of science-fiction gadgetry, it invokes a positive image for American technology.

The best and most important of Gottfredson's foreign tales, however, is "The Monarch of Medioka," a 1939 story of intrigue among the aristocracy of a small Ruritanian kingdom. The story was inspired by the 1937 swashbuckler **The Prisoner of Zenda**, starring Ronald Colman as Rudolph Rassendyll, an Englishman on holiday who helps defeat a rebel conspiracy by impersonating the kidnaped king of Zenda. Gottfredson borrowed liberally from the film: Mickey, like Rudolph, is aided by two court counselors and threatened by a duke bent on becoming king himself—though the main villain in the film is the king's brother, next in line for the throne. And again, like Rudolph, Mickey is caught in an awkward betrothal to a local princess.

At the same time, Gottfredson embellished the story heavily, making it thoroughly his own. He indulged in a penchant for puns by naming the Minister of Finance Count de Sheckels and the canine Secretary of Foreign Affairs, Duke de la Puche. The villainous duke, who sports a pencil-thin mustache and a perpetual snarl, became Duke Varlott. The King, called Michael (probably because this is the formal version of Mickey) acquires a breadth of character lacking in the film. On the screen, there is only a hint that he is a wastrel: he gets drunk at dinner and is upbraided by his chief counselor. In

"Medioka," Michael is a libertine who cares only for parties and whose spendthrift ways have bankrupted the royal treasury. The film revolves merely around a palace plot, but Gottfredson's strip sees broader implications: Michael has taxed his subjects so much to support his playboy lifestyle that they are ready to rebel—incited, of course, by Duke Varlott. Again Gottfredson

Mickey Mouse Is Banned By Censors in Yugoslavia

Wireless to THE NEW YORK TIMES

BELGRADE, Yugoslavia, Dec. 1— Mickey Mouse has fallen under the censor's ban here. The daily comic strip appearing in Politika is now forbidden.

It told the story of how the uncle of a reigning prince became alarmed at the popularity of Mickey—the reigning prince's double—who was substituting for the absent prince. The uncle, seeing that Mickey's popularity was steadily increasing, decided to halt this.

The story had just reached the point where the uncle was organizing a military conspiracy when the censor intervened, forbidding its continuation.

This news story filed by NEW YORK TIMES correspondent Hubert Harrison on December 1, 1937 resulted in his expulsion from Yugoslavia. The *Mickey Mouse* serial mentioned in the dispatch is Floyd Gottfredson's masterpiece, "The Monarch of Medioka."

invoked images of mass poverty and the seizure of power, but this time they occur in Europe.

The tone of Gottfredson's tale is different from that of the film because he introduces a theme missing from the movie. He makes it central: the conflict between Mickey's democratic American

values and Medioka's belief in aristocratic privilege. When a sentry halts Mickey's coach and wants to examine the baggage, the Count becomes furious, calling the man an "insolent puppy" and telling him it is not his business to think. The egalitarian Mickey, on the other hand, props up the guard's self-esteem by praising his dilligence. The guard returns happy to his post, proving that the American way has its points. Again the contrast is made when the real King departs, and the guard mistakenly thanks him for his kind words. Michael takes this as impudence and threatens to have the man horse-whipped, so that the aristocrat comes out of the situation as a brute. This dichotomy between humanitarianism and brutality is most evident in the scene where Mickey halts the King's guards just as they are about to spray the populace with bullets, at his Minister's command.

As America emerged from isolationism, the country began to look upon itself as a redeemer that could make foreign nations over in its own democratic image. This idea was based on what we thought was our exceptional status in world history: we had no feudal tradition to overcome, therefore we constituted a practically pristine Eden, with liberty, equality, and justice for all. Our isolation from the contaminating influence of the old world, the freedom of our great open frontiers, and our heritage of democratic institutions all seemed to make this possible.

We also congratulated ourselves on our empirical and pragmatic cast of mind, evident in the country's rapid taming of a rough frontier and our extensive development of science and technology. Thus Mickey is able to balance the national budget and dispel popular discontent with plain old American know-how. At one stroke, he lowers both the people's taxes and the salaries of his Ministers, an egalitarian solution that efficiently returns Medioka to solvency.

Europeans, on the other hand, we assumed were far too shackled by centuries of tradition to share in America's social vision. Thus the

---

[20] *Richard Pells,* American Visions, American Dreams: Culture and Social Thought in the Depression Years *(New York: Harper and Row, 1973), p. 293.*

THE MICKEY MOUSE CONSPIRACY THAT YUGOSLAVIA BANNED

This strip ran in *The New York Times* **as part of the Yugoslav controversy, a rarity for a newpaper that publishes no comics.**

Mediokans, grateful as they are to Mickey, are shown ready to put him to death for violating a petty custom and sitting on a throne which does not pertain to his common blood. Indeed, King Michael displays his newfound sense of responsibility by expressing himself willing to carry out the sentence, even though he has a personal attachment to Mickey. Our hero is saved only through a trick, the old world being adept in subterfuge: Count de Sheckels has had the foresight to substitute a fake throne for the real one.

Mickey's financial solutions, and his conversion of the country to democracy are, however, only the fantasy of fiction. Michael's conversion occurs too easily: he rides into town in a hay-cart, the people take this as a sign of newfound humility, they cheer him, and he responds to their love with friendship. Not only is the transformation based on a mistake, it seems unlikely, given the strong portrait Gottfredson painted earlier of an arrogant libertine, that the King will shed his tradition of centuries of aristocratic habit in a day. Indeed, Medioka has not actually become a democracy: it has simply traded an insufferable monarch for a benevolent one.

Nonetheless, Gottfredson's portrait of Medioka cut so close to the bone that it was central to the most egregious case of censorship in the strip's history. In December 1937, the Yugoslavian paper **Politika** censored **Mickey Mouse** and the government expelled Hubert Harrison, an American news correspondent who had written a press release about the incident for the **New York Times**. "Monarch of Medioka" had reached the scene in which Varlott begins to conspire against the crown, when the strip was banned for expressing anti-monarchist sentiments.

It was not the last time **Mickey** would be censored. "According to an Italian fan," Gottfredson recalled, "Mussolini, his children, and grandchildren were fans of the **Mickey** strip. During the Second World War, we began to do anti-Axis stories in the strip. Mussolini held off taking it out of the papers until Hitler forced him to censor it. According to this fan, the censorship of the **Mickey** strip caused the beginning of the first youth rebellion against Mussolini."[21]

Troubled Times

Science had advanced significantly in the years following World War I, and as it was turned toward developing more weapons of destruction, it threatened to unleash forms of violence greater than any the world had yet known. In "Island in the Sky," Mickey must confront the existence of an energy source that can obliterate the entire world: atomic power. In 1937, of course, atomic energy and atom bombs were still just the speculations of theoretical physicists and science-fiction writers with active imaginations. Though Gottfredson himself denied any working knowledge of atomic potential, saying he and his writers were just using their imaginations, his was one of the first comic strips to deal with the possibility of atomic power and its destructive potential.

The story was actually inspired by the 1936 film serial **Flash Gordon**, in which King Voltan, monarch of the Hawkmen, has built a fantastic city in the air, suspending it with rays of atomic power. In Gottfredson's comic, Mickey finds a whole island floating in the sky. Wanting to ground the story in some form of reality that would be recognizable to his readers, Gottfredson named the inventor of this miracle Dr. Einmug, a play on words suggesting Einstein, whose theory of relativity was providing a blueprint for the development of atomic energy.

The central question asked by the story is whether the world is ready for atomic power. Pete, as a privateer, intends to sell the weapon for a billion dollars—presumably to the unnamed foreign power that made Einmug a similar offer earlier. Mickey, of course, represents the U.S. attitude: "If my country had it, it'd **stop** wars—on account of anybody else 'ud be scared t' **start** one!" But Einmug is not convinced. He himself is an idealist, obsessively dedicated to guarding his invention and protecting the world. He has even rigged the machinery of the island so that the entire citadel will fall to earth and be destroyed before Pete can obtain the atomic formula. In a scene reminiscent of Voltan's city

---

[21] *Gottfredson interviews.*

For two weeks in May 1931 Gottfredson openly solicited readers to send in a stamped envelope to receive a free autographed "photo" of Mickey. Afterwards, Walt wanted to know whose idea it was, commenting, "Let's get publicity, but for God's sake don't do that again!" There's no documentation as to the volume of mail received.

faltering when his prisoners fail to stoke the atom furnaces, Einmug's island begins to quiver. To increase the excitement, Gottfredson allowed Mickey to restore the island's engines only at the very last second, after a ferocious fistfight with Pete.

The story would seem to end on a note of closure, with the villain subdued and the island in the sky safely afloat once more. But, for once, Mickey does not win the prize he set out to get. Even after he has proven his good intentions to Einmug, the scientist refuses to give him the formula. Gottfredson's message seems to be a pacifist one, with Einmug declaring that atomic energy is too dangerous for any nation to possess.

1939's "The Phantom Blot" (reprinted in this volume) is arguably Gottfredson's finest story; certainly it contains his most memorable villain. The serial appeared only months before World War II erupted; it is suffused with paranoia, revealing how close to home Americans felt the threat had come by this time. No longer could a foreign menace be dealt with simply in foreign lands. The Blot, a sinister agent for a foreign syndicate, operates among us and threatens both our security and the world's.

To make his villain look particularly malevolent, Gottfredson clothed the Blot in a body-length black cloak with only oblong vertical holes for eyes, giving no clue as to who or what lurked beneath. "I had been visualizing a character that looked like that," he commented, "who we could do a mystery with. So my writer suggested a story involving stolen cameras and

a waterfront locale."[22] The Blot's name and the costume were inspired by two black children called "the Blots" in one of the artist's favorite comic strips, Walter Hoban's **Jerry on the Job.** "They were like Siamese twins," Gottfredson recalled, "who moved and talked in unison and were coal black except for their white eyes and lips."[23] In the story Gottfredson only called his character the **Blot,** and all reprints since then have left the name intact. However, in 1940 a comic book was issued that titled the story **Mickey Mouse Outwits the Phantom Blot,** and the name stuck. Fans—and even Gottfredson—tended to refer to the villain as the **Phantom** Blot after that, because like a phantom, the Blot is a ghostly presence, watching and hearing everything we do. We first see him stealthily trailing Mickey, then sitting unobserved in the back of Mickey's cab as the mouse rides to the police station. Gottfredson even adopted the black kids' habit of walking in unison for one panel which shows the Blot creeping in step behind Mickey.[24]

Though the artist drew immediate inspiration from Hoban's characters, the Blot's inky form had been percolating in his mind for years. The Fox, created by Disney for the first strip adventure, was also a black-clad figure, as was the villainous Bat Bandit and the cloaked scientist in "The Mad Doctor," the film cartoon that inspired "Blaggard Castle." Villains dressed all in black had been common film fare since Louis Feuillade's movies about the French terrorist Fantomas, and Gottfredson was clearly fascinated by these shadowy figures.

The fact that the "kindhearted" Blot can never kill in person, instead devising elaborate traps to murder Mickey while he is distanced, makes him particularly diabolical. In effect, his devices are self-destruction machines, designed not just to kill Mickey in his absence, but to make the mouse murder himself. Bound and drugged, with a noose around his neck, Mickey is placed on a high rafter, so that when he falls off, he will hang himself; or his foot is tied to the trigger of a gun, so that when he is forced to move, the weapon will discharge. These devices have roots in the suicide gags in "Mr. Slicker" and Pete and Shyster's rigged shotgun in "The Great Orphanage Robbery," but nobody other than the Blot was so consistently ingenious in meting out deathtraps.

For the Blot, these murder-in-absentia weapons fill an important psychological need: by a kind of twisted reasoning, they absolve him from responsibility, since he is never present when the traps are sprung. For Gottfredson, they solved an editorial problem: "This was done because we couldn't do any killing in the strip. We had to show violence in a tongue-in-cheek way, so we could only go so far."[25] In creating a reason

---

[22] Ibid.

[23] Ibid.

[24] *Gottfredson liked the creeping-in-step gimmick and used it again in 1940 in the western Mickey adventure, "The Bar-None Ranch." It is likely Hoban and Gottfredson had seen this done in vaudeville routines and early movies.*

[25] *Gottfredson interviews.*

for murderous devices that would threaten but never quite kill Mickey, Gottfredson gave the Blot a twisted mind like that of no other villain in the strip, making him a truly frightening adversary.

The final scene imposes a bit of wartime propaganda. Like earlier stories, the tale of the Blot revolves around a great mystery: seemingly worthless cameras are being stolen for no apparent reason. It turns out that the formula concealed in the Blot's camera was stolen from an American firm that intended giving it to hospitals at cost, for the betterment of mankind; but a foreign syndicate wants to adapt it to make war material "more powerful than any known." The United States and her enemies are thus drawn in simple, black-and-white terms as America was girding itself for war.

The decade's end saw a diminution of interest in programs of social reform and a retreat from the ferment of radicalism of the early thirties. By this time, the failures of the New Deal had become apparent and there was growing cynicism about the mushrooming powers of the Roosevelt administration's federal government. The threat of war and facism dampened interest in social experimentation as foreign affairs, rather than domestic issues, became paramount in American's eyes. And the oppressiveness of Stalinism, so evident in the Russian Purge trials, disillusioned those intellectuals who had formerly flirted with socialism.

Indications of these shifts are evident in "The Miracle Master," a story about Mickey's discovery of a magic lamp, which houses a wondrous genie. The story is atypical for Gottfredson and is the only one in which he did not explain away supernatural events, other than to leave the reader wondering if it had all been a dream. It also breaks new ground by showing that although Mickey is well intentioned and performs magnificently good deeds, they all backfire and he is a failure in accomplishing his goals. Thus it considers a possibility never entertained in previous adventures: that one's actions may have unpredictable consequences.

The art and initial premise of "The Miracle Master" was based on the 1940 cartoon, "Pluto's Dream House," in which Mickey digs up a magic lamp. As he had done throughout the late thirties, Gottfredson looked beyond the cartoon and may have been inspired by the H. G. Wells film, **The Man Who Could Work Miracles**. He would also have known of the "Sorcerer's Apprentice" sequence in the yet-to-be-released **Fantasia**, in which Mickey is a hapless magician's helper. In both films, ordinary mortals acquire godly powers with which they are ill-equipped to deal, and their magic spins disastrously out of control. In "The Miracle Master," Mickey, too, is unable to harness his powers at first—but the focus of the story is on people's reactions **to** his magic and **not** his lack of control over it.

Influenced by the conservatism of the times, Gottfredson effectively used the magic theme to satirize liberal programs of social reform. Mickey's decision to stop using his magic for trivial things is a prelude to the mouse artist's critique of liberal environmentalism—the facile assumption that it was not people's living conditions that caused their problems and that they were not responsible for their plight. At this time, films like **Dead End** were claiming that it is slums that breed juvenile delinquency and crime. "Those people are all right!" Mickey proclaims to the genie, "It's just the way they've had to live!"—and he decides to transform the city dump into beautiful, park-laden housing, which he offers rent free to the slum dwellers.

But the result is a liberal reformer's nightmare: the poor are so cynical that they think Mickey is a swindler and they refuse to move into the dwellings. Mickey's attempt to aid the disadvantaged is equally thwarted by local officials. A huge bureaucracy had grown up as a result of Roosevelt's creation of a welfare state, and Gottfredson satirized the way it had so entangled officials in a morass of red tape that they were blind to humanitarian impulses. Instead of congratulating Mickey for his good deed, the police put him in jail for building without a permit. And the mayor himself is more concerned that the city dump is "homeless" than about the lack of good housing for the poor. Gottfredson even parodied New Deal labor unionism by making it seem ludicrously inhibiting. The mayor condemns Mickey for not using local labor—and even the genie is unionized, refusing to perform miracles after his four-hour shift. This reflects the conservative drift at the end of the decade, for in that philosophy, unions were considered restrictive, destroying initiative.

In the end, the mayor and his cronies are just grafters out to use the city's regulations to steal

Mickey's decision to "end it once and for all" in a two-week sequence was Walt Disney's idea. Gottfredson was surprised that it got no negative response from editors or the public.

When Pete's peg leg was dropped in the films, no explanation was ever given to the audiences, but Gottfredson felt "we had to explain it a little bit," so he drew a strip to show "that he'd gotten himself a new artificial leg with a shoe on it."

Mickey's housing project. Gottfredson's story offers a profound examination of the problems involved in the utopian enterprise: it suggests that even if poverty were eliminated, the poor would still be miserable. Having been told by the genie that they would appreciate his philanthropy, Mickey makes all the citizens of Genieland rich. However, although they had been starving, living in ramshackle houses and wearing patched clothing, they are not only **ungrateful**, they are incensed by Mickey's gifts. Gottfredson painted an unsympathetic portrait: although the genies possess magic powers they do not have the capacity to help themselves, and are peevish cranks who complain about whatever they get. They chase Mickey out of town and threaten to boil him in oil, for now that they have everything, they believe they have nothing left to live for.

This is a brilliant satire of the paradoxes and contradictions in building a utopian society. We might do well to compare "The Miracle Master" with "The Great Orphanage Robbery," in which Mickey is not only efficacious in helping the poor, but is a symbol of hope for all those in need. We see how far Gottfredson and his America had traveled since the early thirties.

The Final Continuities

In June 1943, Frank Reilly was hired to take over from Gottfredson as head of the comic strip department. Now freed from those chores, Gottfredson was able to ink his own strip, which he continued to do until his retirement. At the same time, writer Bill Walsh was hired to script **Mickey Mouse** and Gottfredson was no longer

involved in plotting the last twelve years of continuities. Walsh changed the strip's flavor dramatically, introducing zany, almost surreal humor and a dark, gothic tone. His stories—populated with spooks, zombies, and even sea serpents—relect the disillusionment of the war years and the mounting tensions of the early fifites, as America moved toward an uncertain future in the nuclear age.

The **Mickey** adventures had seen their heyday, and in the mid-fifties, King Features once again requested a change in the daily. This time it returned to the gag-a-day formula because of the syndicate's belief that this would enable newspapers to compete with the instant gratification offered by television. The change in format spelled a transformation in Mickey as well. No longer an intrepid adventurer, he became a sedate suburbanite who rarely ventured outside his own neighborhood.

But Mickey had already begun to evolve into a less energetic character in the late thirties. By the next decade his youthful exuberence, symbolized by his shoe-button eyes, short red pants and oversize shoes, had given way to an even more humanized and contemporary mouse sporting polo shirts and slacks—stolidly middle class and clearly "adult." Although Gottfredson wanted to return to an adventure format and felt that its loss diminished the popularity of the strip, he wholeheartedly embraced the changes in Mickey's appearance. In a 1968 interview with Disney collector Malcolm Willits, he defended the position that the contemporary Mickey was artistically superior to his predecessor. "Now his figure is streamlined and shows more sophis-

tication [and] the drawing flows more. In the 1930s...Mickey's figure was crude, anatomically bad, bumpy, stodgy....I shudder to look at work I did during that period."[26]

After he retired, Gottfredson became more tempered in his judgment about the old Mickey, and often expressed a nostalgic fondness for the early adventure stories.

"When I first saw the pupils in Mickey's eyes in model sheets in 1938, I liked it immediately, although it was hard for me to do for awhile until I got used to it. I would like to see a compromise now: a streamlined Mickey but with a pixieish personality. I always felt that Mickey should have been a little [Charlie] Chaplin mouse against the world and I tried to promote that idea when they dropped the continuity and started the...gag-a-day strips. Mickey had become bland and wishy-washy, too much like Dagwood and Blondie, in the neighborhood format. But my idea for changing Mickey's personality was rejected."[27]

Gottfredson lived until 1986, long enough to see his early works reprinted in books, magazines and comics all over the world. The present collection will enable fans, old and new, to meet Mickey in the years of his greatest glories. Gottfredson himself, whose name was once known only to a handful of insiders, will be remembered as one of the small pantheon of artists who were the shining lights of comics' golden age.

---

[26] *Quoted in Malcolm Willits, "An Interview with Floyd Gottfredson," Vanguard, No. 2 (February 1968), p. 28.*

[27] *Gottfredson interviews.*

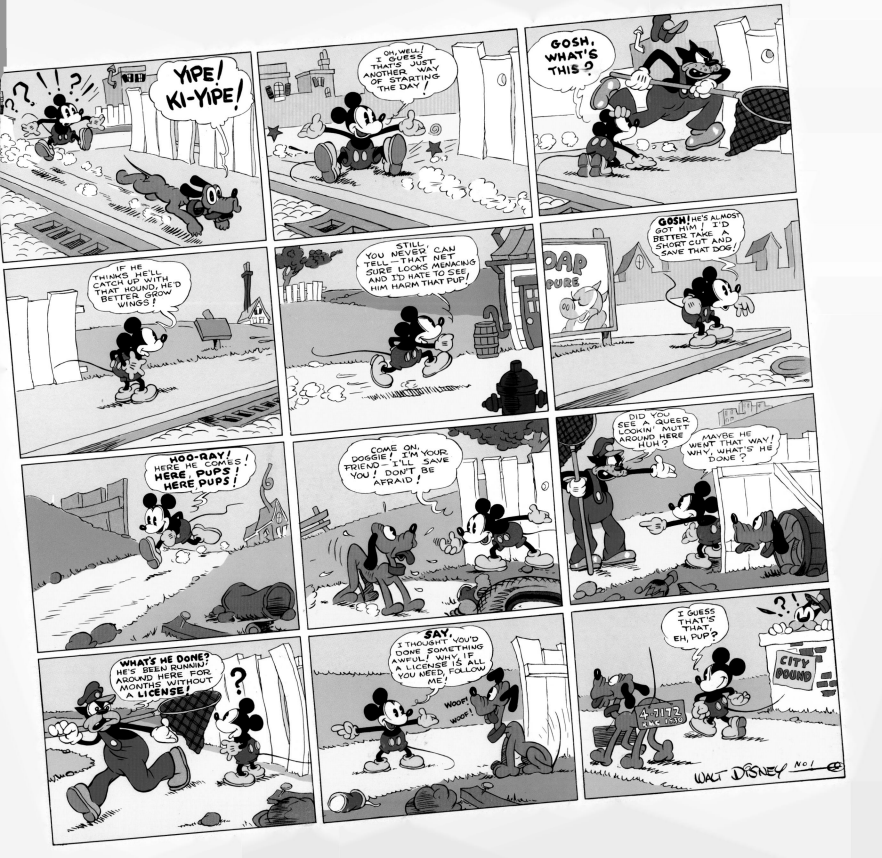

WALT DISNEY N01

5/15/32

7/31/32

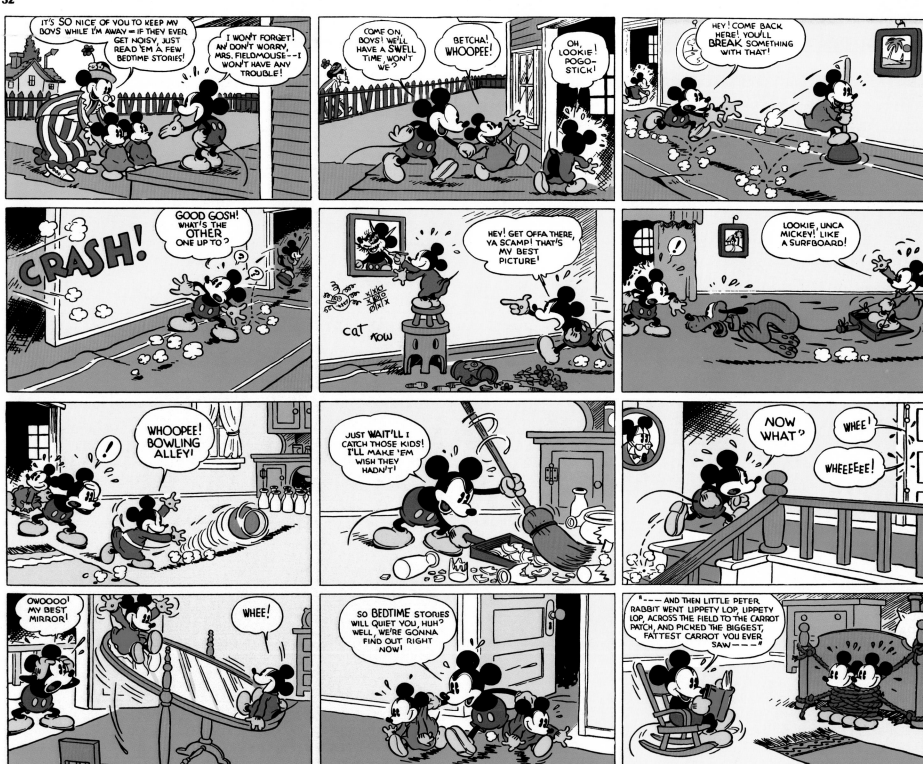

7/9/33

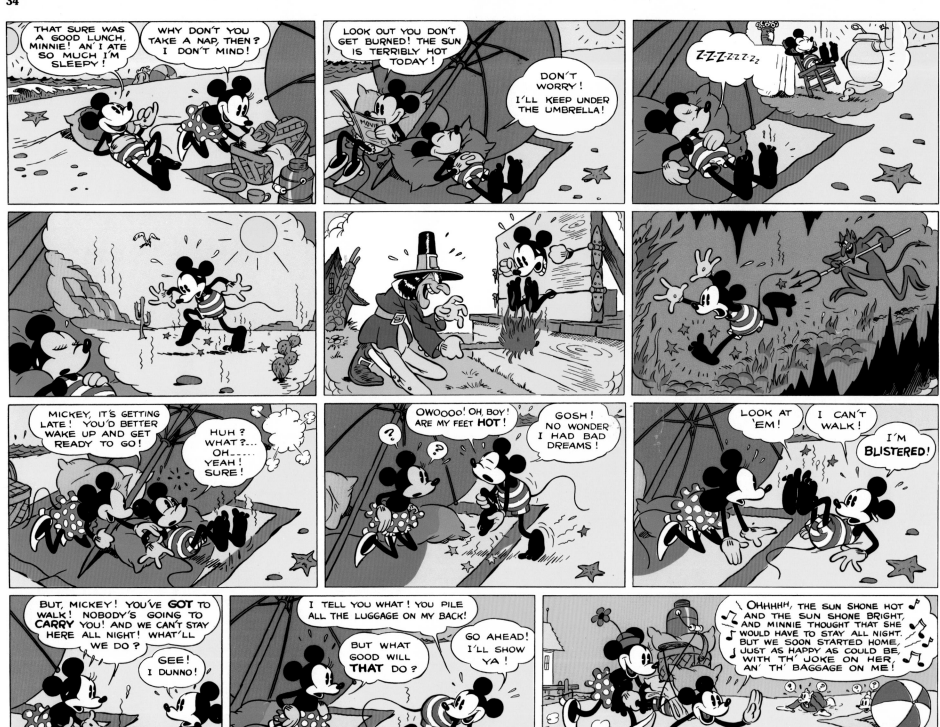

MICKEY MOUSE

and

RUMPLEWATT THE GIANT

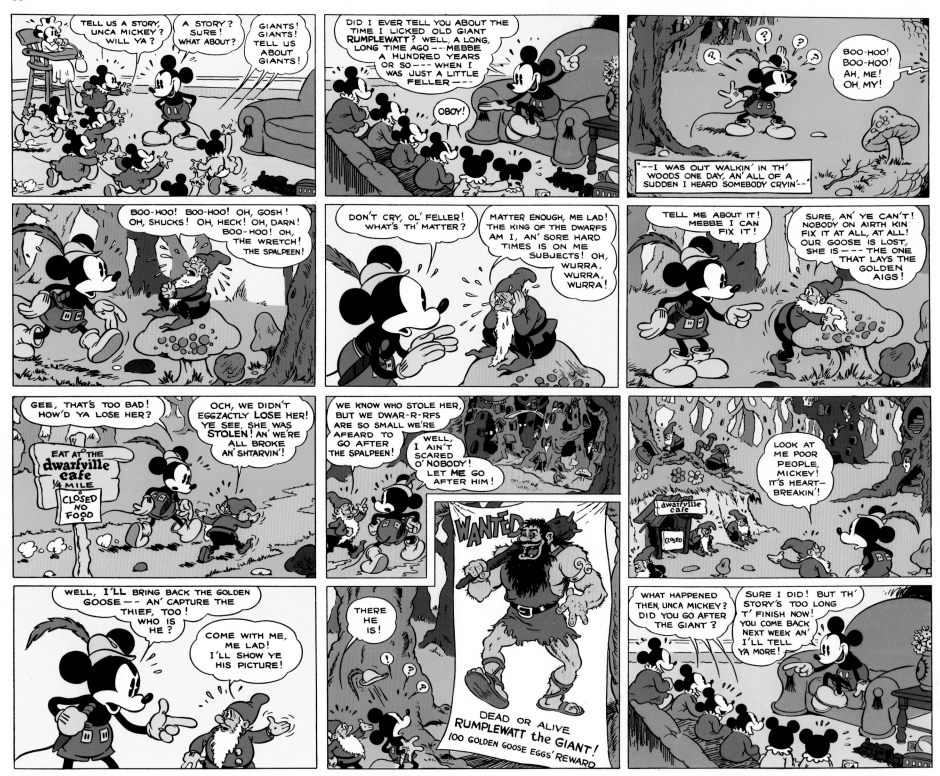

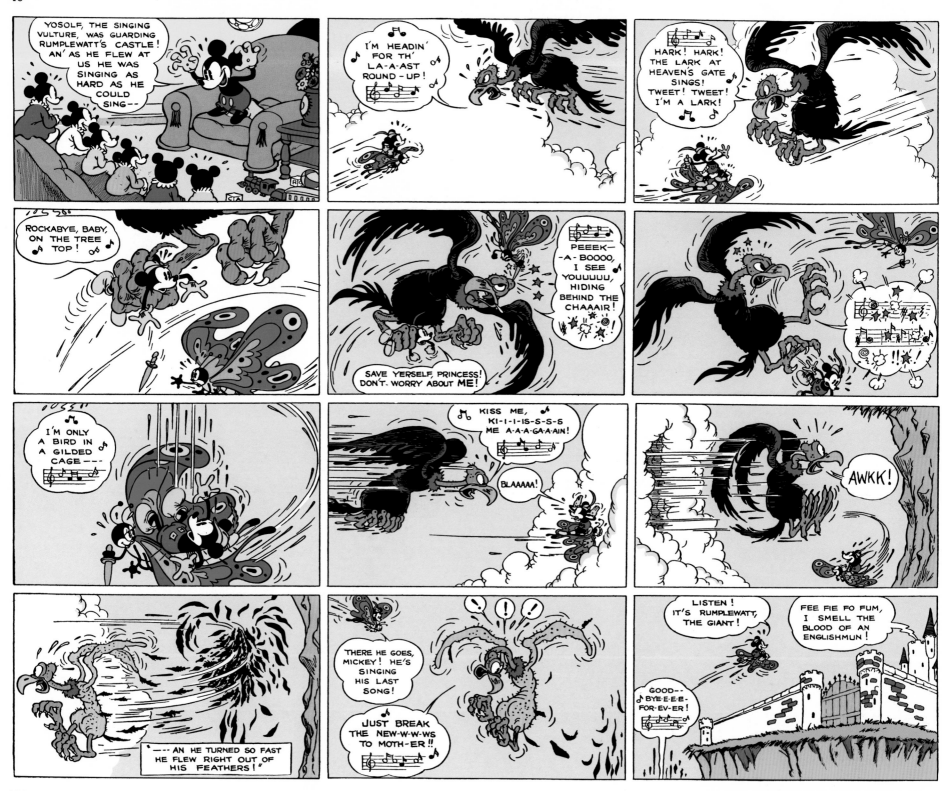

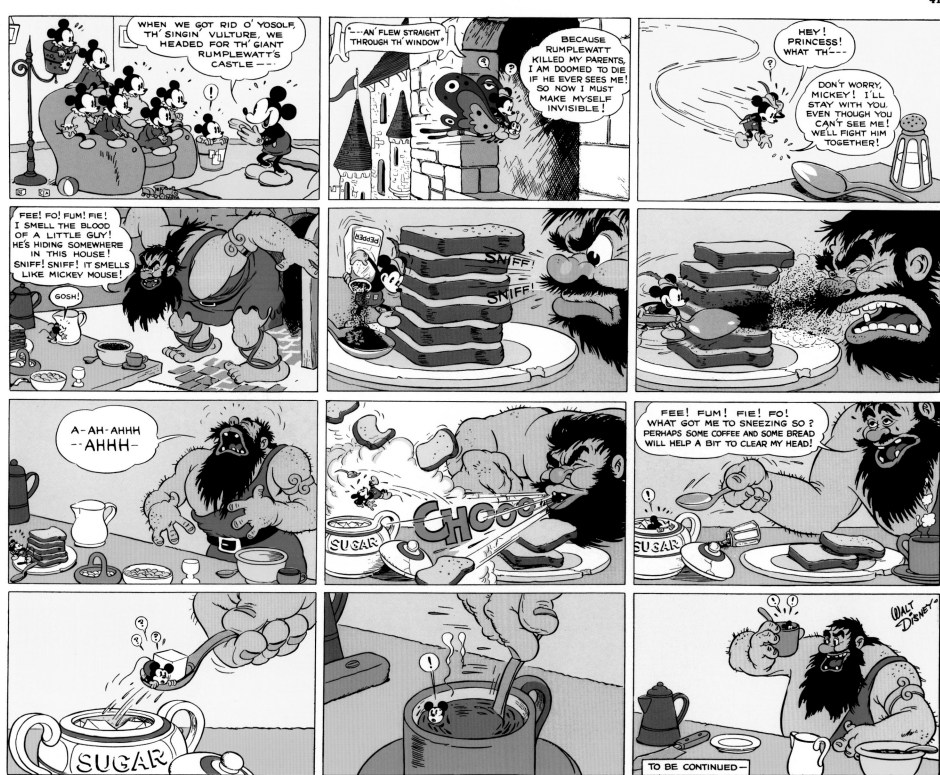

42

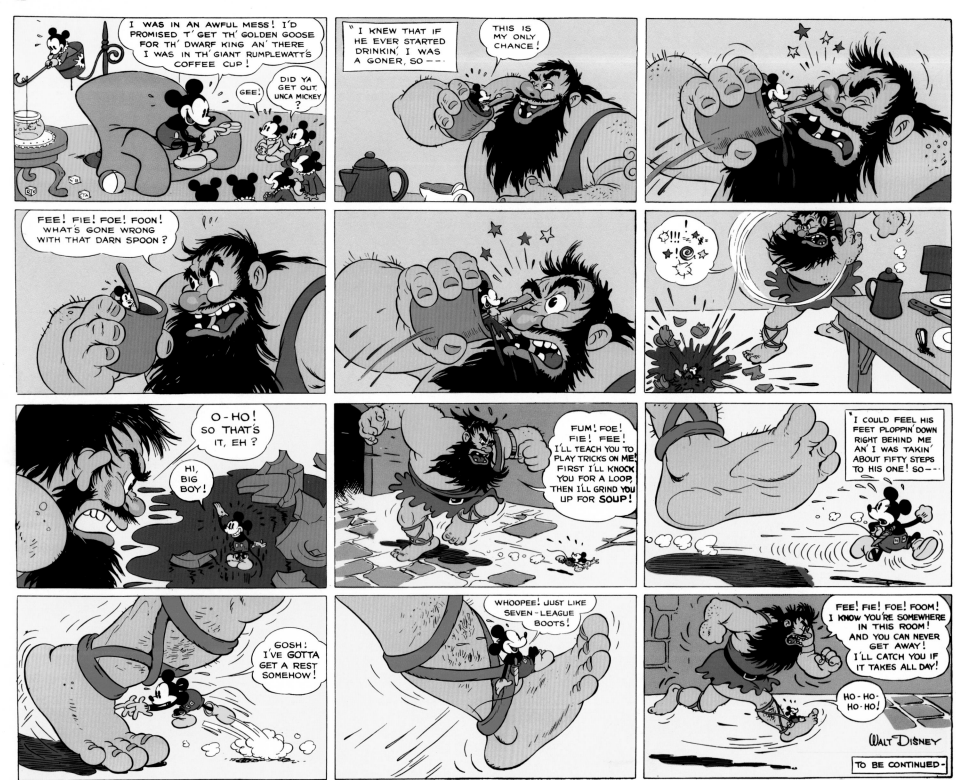

4/8/34

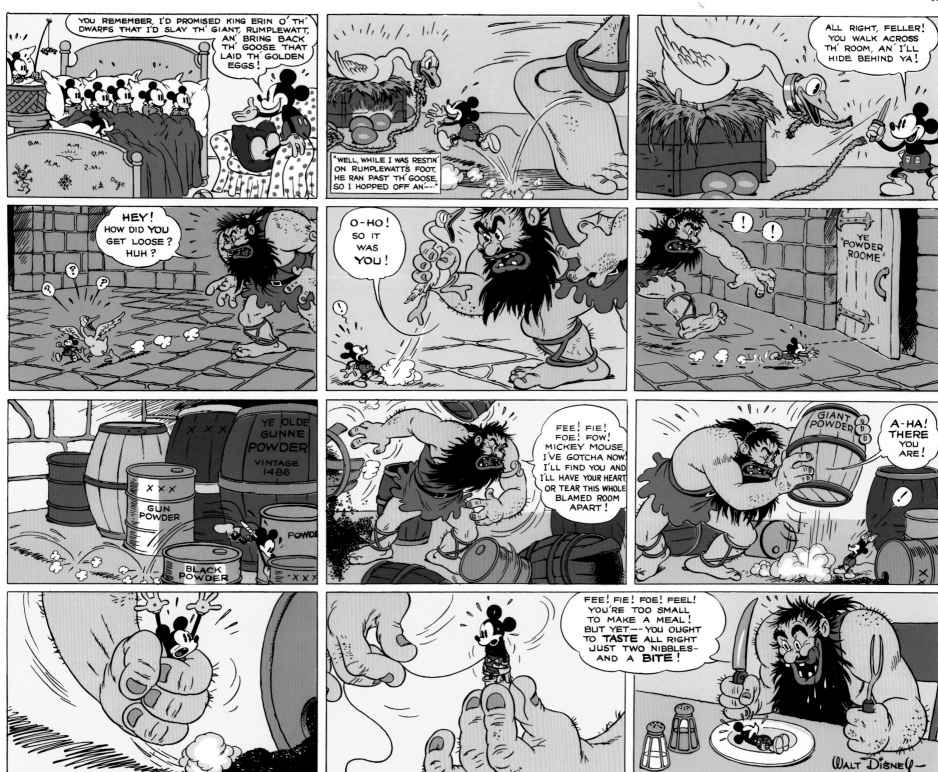

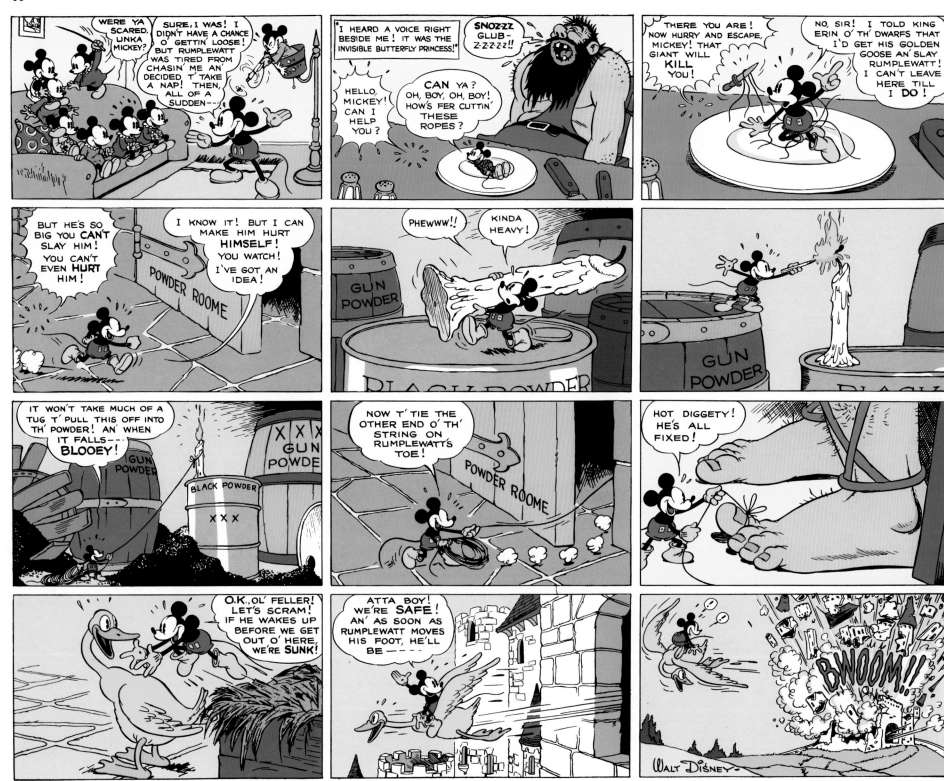

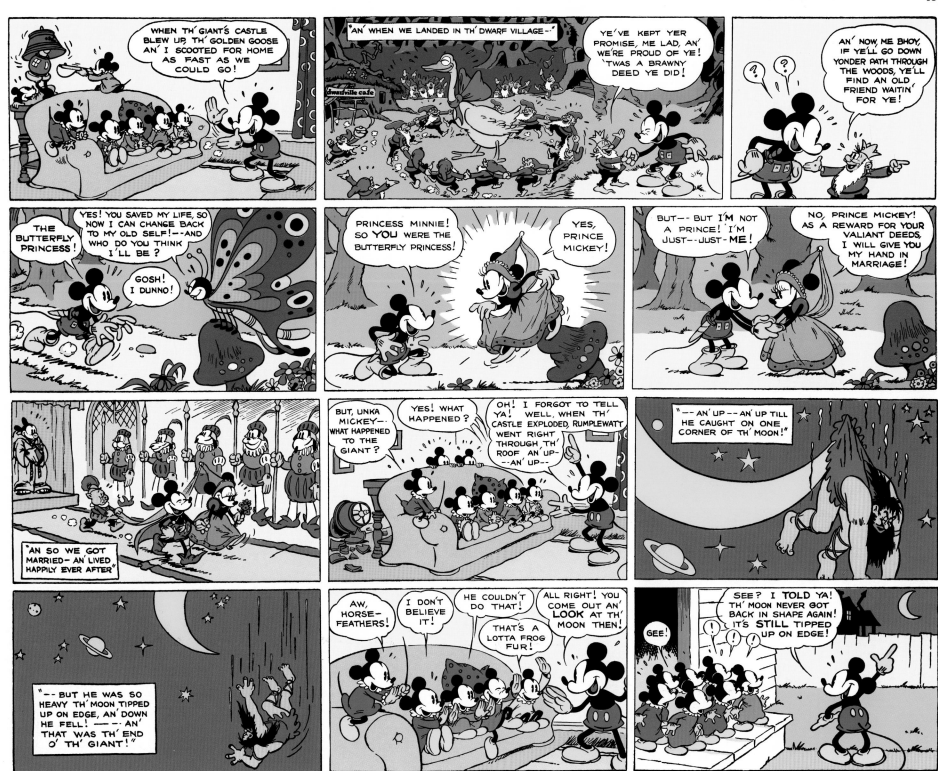

MICKEY MOUSE

and

DR. OOFGAY'S SECRET SERUM

48

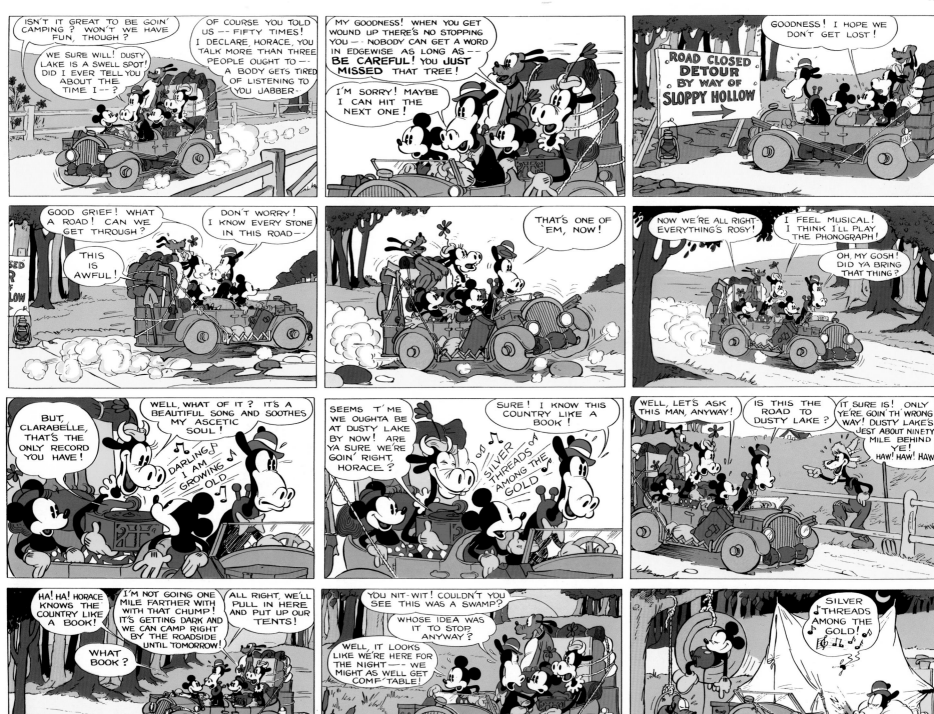

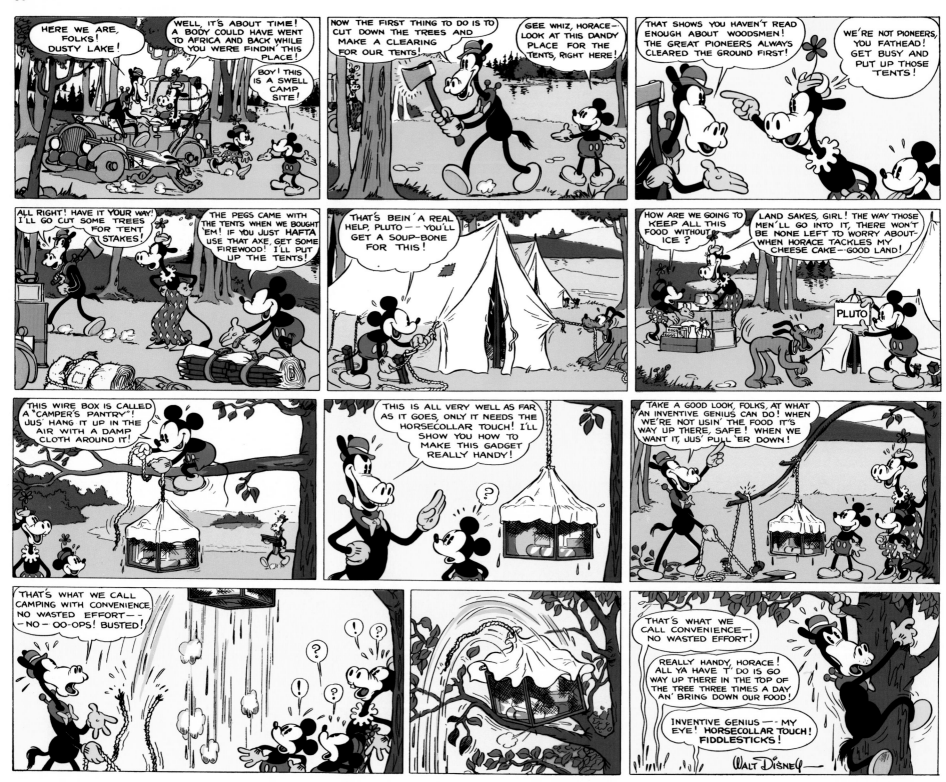

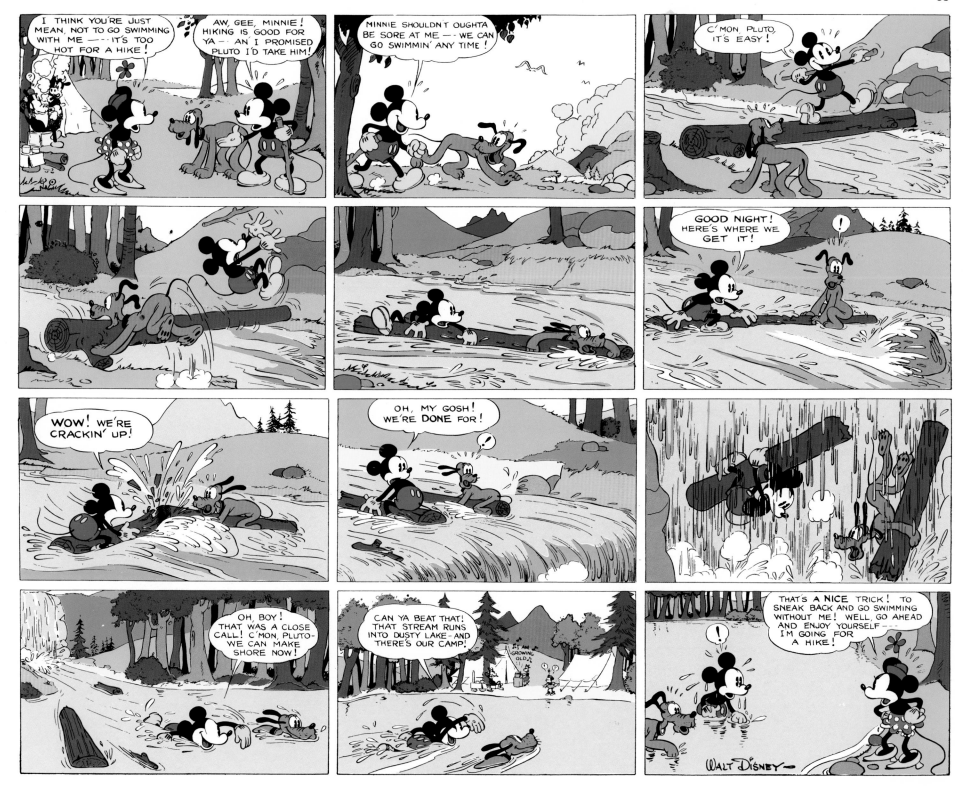

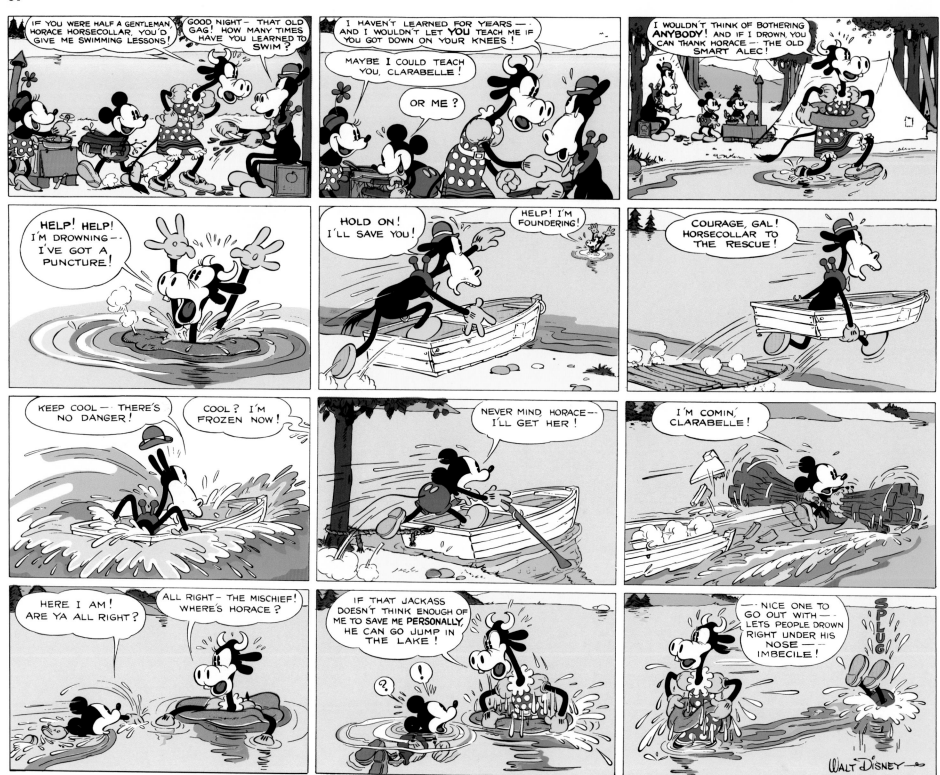

8/12/34

9/9/34

11/25/34

MICKEY MOUSE

and

DONALD DUCK

in

THE CASE OF THE VANISHING COATS

64

65

2/24/35

68

3/17/35

EIGHT O'CLOCK THE NEXT NIGHT!

3/24/35

MICKEY MOUSE

THE ROBIN HOOD
ADVENTURE

the ROBIN HOOD

LOOK AT TH' SPINDLY THING! ALL MY FLOWERS ARE THAT WAY! DOGGONE IT, I WISH THERE WAS SOME KIND O' PLANT FOOD THAT 'UD—

BY GOLLY! TH' PAPERS ARE FULL OF ADS ABOUT TONICS AN' VITAMINS AN' STUFF! I WONDER WHAT WOULD HAPPEN IF—

GIMME ONE OF EVERY KIND O' TONIC YOU'VE GOT! BODY-BUILDERS—THAT'S WHAT I WANT! STUFF T' MAKE YA BIG AN' STRONG!

BOY! IF JUST ONE O' THESE WILL WORK ON PEOPLE, THINK HOW A HUNDRED OF 'EM WILL WORK ON FLOWERS!

THERE! AN' IF THIS DOESN'T GROW 'EM, I'M GONNA GIVE UP!

WELL—THERE'S ONLY ONE WAY T' FIND OUT! AN' THEN, IN A COUPLE O' DAYS—

WELL, I'LL BE—IT'S—IT'S BEGINNIN' T' WORK ALREADY!

HOT DIGGETTY! LOOK AT IT GO!

WELL, FER—NOW IT'S GETTIN' TOO BIG! I GUESS MEBBE I'D BETTER STOP IT!

BOY! THAT STUFF SURE MUST BE STRONG!

HEY! WHAT TH'—

WELL, F' GOSH SAKES!

TO BE CONTINUED—

ADVENTURE

5/3/36

the ROBIN HOOD

ADVENTURE

the ROBIN HOOD

WHILE EXPERIMENTING WITH HIS MAGIC PLANT TONICS, MICKEY ACCIDENTALLY SPRAYS SOME "REDUCER" ON HIMSELF— AND SHRINKS TO ALMOST NOTHING!

HERE, PLUTO! C'MON, BOY!

I DON'T BLAME YER FOR BEIN' SURPRISED! I FEEL SORT O' FUNNY, MYSELF!

!

BUT YOU LET ME DOWN ON TH' FLOOR BY TH' TONIC, AN' I'LL MAKE MYSELF BIG AGAIN!

OH, F'GOSH SAKES! I FORGOT ALL ABOUT THAT FLY I FIXED UP!

HUZZZ! SOZZ YEZ ROZZ!

ZIZZIFIZIZ ZZZ WOZZZ-Z-Z-Z!

BRRRRR!

R-ROW-OOO!

LOOK AT HIM! HE'S LAFFIN' AT YA!

WOZZ WOZZ WOZZ WOZZ WOZZ!

ATTA BOY, PLUTO! SIC 'IM! GO GET 'IM, BOY!

AR-RRRR!

ZOZZ OWZZ! OZZ SOZZ YEZ WOZZ!

OWOOOOO!

!

TO BE CONTINUED

ADVENTURE

ITH A HUGE FLY CHASING HIM AND A REDUCED MICKEY HOLDING ONTO HIS TAIL, POOR PLUTO IS TERRIFIED!

OF ALL TH' SILLY PICKLES T' BE IN! IF I WAS SOMEBODY ELSE, I'D PROB'LY BUST MYSELF LAUGHIN' AT ME!

BUT IT'S NO LAUGHIN' MATTER—TILL I GET BACK TO TH' BASEMENT AN' MAKE MYSELF BIG AGAIN!

GR-RRR-R-RRR!

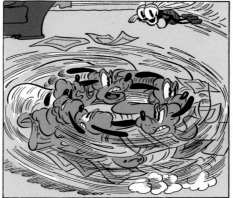

WUZZ! WUZZ! WOZZ! WOZZ! WOZZ!

ZUZZ YEZ WUZZ, ZOZZ!

WOP!

F'GOSH SAKES! NOW I AM IN A JAM! WITH PLUTO GONE, HOW'LL I EVER GET DOWN OFF O' THIS TABLE?

SOZZ! YUZZ ZOZZ, HUZZ! WOZZ!

!

TO BE CONTINUED—

the ROBIN HOOD

ADVENTURE

6/14/36

the ROBIN HOOD

WHILE HIDING IN A ROBIN HOOD BOOK, MICKEY IS CAPTURED BY SOME OF THE ILLUSTRATIONS AND TAKEN BEFORE THE SHERIFF OF NOTTINGHAM!

SIRE, WE HAVE TWO PRISONERS! ..THIS ONE WE CAUGHT POACHING ON HIS MAJESTY'S DEER!

TO THE GIBBET WITH HIM! HANG HIM AT ONCE!

AND THE OTHER?

HE IS A BALMY VARLET THE CHIEF FORESTER FOUND LURKING IN SHERWOOD FOREST!

SPEAK, KNAVE! WHO ART THOU, AND WHENCE CAMEST THOU?

I'M MICKEY MOUSE, AN' I JUST SORTA DROPPED IN ON YA FROM TH' TWENTIETH CENTURY!

I KNOW NOT THAT PLACE! WHERE IS IT LOCATED?

WELL — IT'S LOCATED PRACTICALLY EVERYWHERE— ABOUT A THOUSAND YEARS FROM NOW!

SO! THOU KIDDEST ME, DOST THOU? TO THE DUNGEON WITH YOU! THOU SHALT BE FED TO THE DOGS!

OH, YEAH?

LISTEN, YOU OLD FOSSIL! GET FRESH WITH ME AN' I'LL TEAR YA RIGHT OUT O' TH' BOOK! I NEVER DID LIKE YA, ANYHOW!

ENOUGH! AWAY WITH HIM! HANG HIM WITH THE OTHER KNAVE!

F' GOSH SAKES! I DON'T REMEMBER THIS CHAPTER! I'VE GOTTA THINK O' SOMETHIN' QUICK!

LOOK! THAT PEDDLER! IT'S ROBIN HOOD— IN DISGUISE!

AFTER HIM, MEN!

HOT DIGGETTY! IT WORKED! NOW'S OUR CHANCE!

C'MON! CLIMB ABOARD!

NICE WORK, LAD! THAT WAS A NEAT TRICK! WHAT IS THY NAME?

MICKEY MOUSE!

I AM GLAD, INDEED, TO KNOW THEE! MINE IS ROBIN HOOD!

ADVENTURE

Rescuing a beggar from the Sheriff of Nottingham, Mickey is amazed to find that he is really ROBIN HOOD!

THY QUICK WIT SAVED MY LIFE, LAD! AND I HAVE BUT ONE WAY TO REPAY THEE!

IF THOU WILT SERVE ME AND ENTER MY COMPANY OF MERRY MEN, I WILL PAY THEE WELL! WHAT SAYEST THOU?

OH, BOY! OH, BOY! I SAYEST IT'S SWELL!

HULLOA MY COMRADES!

LOOK!

'TIS ROBIN HOOD!

OUR MASTER HAS TURNED BEGGAR!

A CLATTERING TINSMITH, ON MY HONOR!

CLATTER! KLANK!

BUT WHAT MANNER OF CREATURE IS THIS?

A STRANGE-LOOKING URCHIN!

METHINKS HE IS A FOREIGNER! CANST THOU SPEAK, GAMIN?

SURE! I'M A NEW MAN IN YER GANG!

A NEW MAN? HAW! HAW! HAW!

AN INFANT! A MERE, PULING INFANT!

IF YOU ARE A MAN, LITTLE ONE, I WOULD FAIN TEST THY STRENGTH! SMITE ME ON THE JOWLS!

WELL— IF THAT'S TH' WAY Y' WANT T' PLAY— O.K.!

SMACK!

SO! AND NOW IT IS MY TURN TO SMITE THEE!

NAY! STAY THY HAND! THOU ASKED FOR IT, METHINKS!

LET HIM COME, TH' BIG PALOOKA! I CAN TAKE CARE OF MYSELF!

VERY WELL! SO BE IT! THEY SHALL FIGHT WITH LONG-STAVES TILL ONE CAN FIGHT NO LONGER! MICKEY MOUSE AND LITTLE JOHN!

LITTLE JOHN! OH, F' GOSH SAKES!

6/28/36

the ROBIN HOOD

AVING BEEN ACCEPTED IN ROBIN HOOD'S BAND, MICKEY MUST PROVE HIMSELF BY FIGHTING LITTLE JOHN!

ADVENTURE

On a lazy afternoon in Sherwood Forest, Mickey and the other Merry Men persuade Robin Hood to give an exhibition with his bow and arrow!

7/12/36

the ROBIN HOOD

I'VE READ A LOT ABOUT YER GANG, ROBIN HOOD, BUT TH' BOOKS DON'T SAY MUCH ABOUT HOW YA SPEND YER TIME WHEN YER NOT BUSY!

THERE'S ALWAYS PLENTY TO DO!

"FRIAR TUCK AND LITTLE JOHN KEEP IN TRIM BY FRIENDLY BATTLING! THE LOSER GETS A GOOD DUCKING!"

"OTHERS ENGAGE IN ALL MANNER OF SPORTS — SHOOTING, WRESTLING AND JUMPING!"

"WHILE OTHERS FASHION NEW ARROWS AND MEND CLOTHES TORN BY BRUSH OR BY ARROWS THAT NARROWLY MISSED THEIR MARK!"

WHONN-N-N-NNK!

AH! BUT COME! 'TIS TIME FOR DINNER!

AS THE NEWEST MEMBER OF OUR BAND, THOU WILT SIT IN THE PLACE OF HONOR — ON MY RIGHT HAND!

WHAT'S THE IDEA O' TH' BOWS AN' ARROWS?

'TIS SIMPLE! IN SHERWOOD FOREST WE HAVE NO SERVANTS TO PASS THE FOOD!

A MAN MUST NEEDS GET HIS OWN! I'LL SHOW THEE!

SEE? HERE THOU ART! THE FATTEST PHEASANT ON THE PLATTER!

BOY! THIS IS MY IDEA OF A SWELL WAY T' LIVE!

YES, BUT THOU HAST NOT SEEN THE BEST FUN OF ALL! FOR **REAL** SPORT WAIT UNTIL THIS AFTERNOON!

WHAT SPORT IS THAT?

HOLDING UP AND ROBBING FAT TRAVELERS ON THE PUBLIC HIGHWAYS!

ADVENTURE

the ROBIN HOOD

IT HARDLY SEEMS FAIR T' BEAT A GUY UP AN' THEN ROB 'IM! I'D MUCH RATHER YA'D JUST GIMME YER MONEY— AN' LET IT GO AT THAT!

OH, THAT'S ALL RIGHT! DON'T APOLOGIZE! I REALLY ENJOY FIGHTING!

CONTINUED—

OKAY! HAVE AT YA!

THOU SWINGEST A WICKED QUARTERSTAFF FOR ONE SO SMALL!

CRACK! WHOP! POPPETY POP!

ROBIN HOOD MUST BE VERY PROUD, INDEED, TO HAVE SO VALIANT A FIGHTER IN HIS BAND!

POP WHACK! SOCK!

I DO NOT SUPPOSE THERE IS A SQUIRREL OR RABBIT IN ALL SHERWOOD FOREST THAT COULD STAND AGAINST THEE!

SO! SMARTIN' OFF WITH ME, EH? WELL— LET'S SEE YA STOP THIS ONE!

I REMEMBER ONCE WHEN I FOUGHT LITTLE JOHN! REMIND HIM OF IT SOME TIME! HE WILL BE GLAD TO SHOW YOU THE SCARS!

CRACK

WOP!

GOSH! I'M SORRY! ARE YA HURT?

NOT MUCH! JUST SURPRISED!

IN TWENTY YEARS OF FIGHTING, HERE AND AGAINST THE SARACENS, I HAVE NEVER BEFORE RECEIVED AN UPPERCUT FROM A DOWNWARD BLOW!

HERE, MY LAD! TAKE THE MONEY! THOU HAST EARNED IT! THE LESSON IS CHEAP AT THE PRICE!

ADVENTURE

HERE, MY LAD! TAKE THE MONEY! THOU HAST ROBBED ME FAIRLY AND SQUARELY!

OH, GOSH! I DON'T NEED THAT MUCH!

YA SEE, I'M NOT REALLY A ROBBER! SO ALL I WANT IS ENOUGH T' MAKE ROBIN HOOD **THINK** I AM!

VERY WELL! LET US DIVIDE! EACH SHALL TAKE HALF!

ARE YA SURE THAT ISN'T TOO MUCH? I WANTA BE ABSOLUTELY FAIR ABOUT IT, YA KNOW!

TAKE IT — AND WELCOME! TO PROVE MY GOOD WILL I SHALL GIVE THEE A NOTE TO ROBIN HOOD!

THERE! TAKE THIS TO THY MASTER! HE IS — SHALL I SAY? — A FRIEND OF MINE!

GEE! THAT'S SURE NICE OF YA!

WELL — SO LONG! I HOPE I DIDN'T HURT YA TOO MUCH!

NOT AT ALL! THE PLEASURE HATH BEEN ALL MINE! FAREWELL, MY FRIEND!

I DON'T KNOW WHO THAT GUY IS, BUT HE'S SURE A SWELL EGG! MEBBE I SHOULD'VE ASKED 'IM T' JOIN TH' GANG!

HERE YA ARE, ROBIN HOOD! NOT BAD FOR A BEGINNER, HUH?

BY MY TROTH! 'TIS GOLD! WHOM DIDST THOU ROB — SOME RICH, FAT MERCHANT?

NO, SIR! I GOT IT FROM A **KNIGHT**! I BEAT UP ON HIM AN' HE HANDED IT OVER! WHAT'S MORE, HERE'S A LETTER TO PROVE IT!

F' GOSH SAKES! WHAT'S TH' MATTER?

THIS LETTER! LISTEN!

"THIS MAN DEFEATED ME IN FAIR COMBAT! HE IS A GALLANT FIGHTER AND A CREDIT TO YOUR BAND! BUT I COMMAND THAT NEVER AGAIN SHALL HE BE SENT TO ROB WAYFARERS!"

HE COMMANDS? WHO IS IT THAT —

RICHARD, THE LION-HEARTED! KING OF ALL BRITAIN!

the ROBIN HOOD

8/16/36

ADVENTURE

Seeking further adventures, Mickey decides to try rescuing a maiden in distress.

Robin Hood warns him of the danger —

But leads him to a castle in which Lady Minerva is held!

DRAW AND DEFEND YERSELVES

WHY? ARE WE BEING ATTACKED?

I'VE COME TO RESCUE A MAIDEN IN DISTRESS!

OH, IS **THAT** ALL? WHY DIDN'T YOU SAY SO? YOU HAD ME WORRIED FOR A MINUTE!

SIR BAFFLEBRANE WILL SHOW YOU TO HER ROOM! AND IF YOU WANT TO FIGHT ON THE WAY, JUST FOR THE FUN OF IT, HERE IS A SWORD!

YA MEAN YER NOT GONNA TRY T' STOP ME?

NO! WHY SHOULD WE? I'M SURE MAID MINERVA WOULD BE DELIGHTED!

RIGHT THIS WAY, MY FRIEND!

I DON'T GET THIS! SHE'S IN DISTRESS, ISN'T SHE?

OF COURSE! BUT SHE WAS IN DISTRESS BEFORE SHE CAME HERE! THAT'S WHY WE'RE HOLDING HER!

WHAT'S SHE DISTRESSED ABOUT?

SHE WANTS TO GET MARRIED! ALL WOMEN DO! AND WHEN THEY GET HARD UP, THEY STAY IN DURANCE VILE UNTIL SOME SAP COMES ALONG AND RESCUES THEM!

Ye Maiden in Distress

WELL — HERE WE ARE! GO RIGHT ON IN!

HEY! WAIT A MINUTE! DO YA MEAN IF I RESCUE HER SHE'LL WANT T' **MARRY** ME?

Ye Durance VILE

WHY — OF COURSE! NOT ONLY THAT, YOU **HAVE** TO MARRY HER! IT'S THE CUSTOM!

CUSTOM BE HANGED! YA DON'T CATCH **ME** RESCUIN' A DIZZY, LOVESICK DAME LIKE THAT!

NOT SO FAST! YOU HAVE COME TOO FAR TO BACK OUT! EITHER YOU RESCUE HER — OR YOU'LL ANSWER TO **ME!**

OH, FER GOSH SAKES!

NOW I KNOW WHY ROBIN HOOD SAID THIS RESCUIN' STUFF WAS SO DANGEROUS!

8/23/36

the ROBIN HOOD

ADVENTURE

Panel 1: MINNIE! WHAT ARE **YOU** DOIN' IN THIS CASTLE? I WAS EXPECTIN' T' FIND A MAIDEN IN DISTRESS!

IN THE FIRST PLACE, DON'T CALL ME "MINNIE"! MY NAME IS MAID MINERVA!

Panel 2: AND DO YOU THINK THAT IS ANY WAY FOR A HERO TO SPEAK TO THE LADY HE IS RESCUING? I WANT YOU TO KNOW I **AM** IN DISTRESS!

WELL — THAT MAKES **TWO** OF US!

Panel 3: DO YA MEAN T' TELL ME YA AREN'T MINNIE MOUSE? AN' YA DON'T **KNOW** ME?

OF COURSE NOT! I AM MAID MINERVA RHODANT — AND I NEVER SAW YOU BEFORE!

Panel 4: WELL, I'LL BE A COCKEYED SO-AN'-SO! THEN — YA MUST BE ONE OF HER **ANCESTORS**!

Panel 5: OHHHHH! OF ALL THINGS! CALLING ME AN **ANCESTOR**! I NEVER WAS SO INSULTED IN ALL MY LIFE!

Panel 6: I'M **NOBODY'S** ANCESTOR — AND I WOULDN'T LET YOU RESCUE ME NOW IF YOU WERE THE LAST MAN ON EARTH!

Panel 7: WELL — OKAY! IF **THAT'S** TH' WAY YA FEEL ABOUT IT, LET'S JUST FORGET TH' WHOLE THING! I'D RATHER, ANYHOW!

Panel 8: BUT — YOU'RE **NOT** THE LAST MAN ON EARTH! AND YOU **HAVE** RESCUED ME! SO — I FORGIVE YOU!

Panel 9: I KNOW YOU WOULDN'T HAVE COME FOR ME IF YOU HADN'T LOVED ME — AND WANTED TO MARRY ME!

WAIT A MINUTE! YOU'RE SURE TAKIN' A LOT FOR GRANTED!

Panel 10: ASK ME THE QUESTION! DON'T BE BASHFUL, MY HERO! WHISPER SWEET NOTHINGS IN MY EARS! I LOVE IT!

HEY! LISTEN! GET AWAY FROM ME! I TELL YA, I —

Panel 11: HOORAY! THE BRIDE AND GROOM!

SHE IS **SAVED**!

WE'RE GONNA HAVE A WEDDING! HERE COMES THE BRIDE!

9/6/36

the ROBIN HOOD

ADVENTURE

9/20/36

the ROBIN HOOD

BOY! WHAT A SPOT! ROBIN HOOD AN' HIS WHOLE GANG, THREE KNIGHTS AN' KING RICHARD, HIMSELF— ALL AFTER ME!

MY ONLY CHANCE NOW IS T' GET TO THAT PICTURE WHERE I CAME INTO THIS DOGGONE BOOK!

YOWIE! THAT WAS CLOSE! IF I DON'T REACH IT PRETTY SOON, IT'LL BE—

HOT DIGGETTY! THERE IT IS!

HE'S ESCAPING! STOP—AND ALL SHOOT AT ONCE! A PRIZE TO THE ARCHER WHO BRINGS HIM DOWN!

SHOOT!

WHEW! WHAT A CLOSE ONE THAT WAS! AN' TH' FUNNY PART OF IT IS, I CAN'T TELL ANYBODY ABOUT IT— 'CAUSE NOBODY'D EVER BELIEVE ME!

ADVENTURE

10/4/36

MICKEY MOUSE

THE MAN WHO DREW THE MOUSE

An Interview with Floyd Gottfredson
by David R. Smith

When I first started preliminary work in 1969 which led to the establishment of the Archives at the Disney Studio, I naturally looked up all of the old-timers I could locate, because the stories about the earliest days of the company were the most difficult to find. It pleased me immensely to discover that some of the Disney employees who had been around the longest were among the friendliest and most personable. Some were a little reticent to confide in a newcomer like myself, but as they began to perceive the value of the Archives, they began to talk and recount great stories about the "good old days." There was Roy O. Disney, who had been around the longest. There was Ub Iwerks, who helped Walt create Mickey Mouse. But probably the greatest gentleman of them all was Floyd Gottfredson. Unlike Roy and Ub, Floyd did not start with the company at its birth—he actually arrived on the scene about six years after the company's beginnings—but he played a major role in getting the new character, Mickey Mouse, known throughout the world by producing the **Mickey Mouse** comic strip. Floyd always had the time to answer my questions and seemed to be a wealth of knowledge about the early days. As opposed to some of the others, his memory was sharp and seemed impeccable. He alone, for example, was able to give me a detailed description of the physical set-up of the Disney Studio in 1929. When Floyd announced his retirement in 1975, I knew that I would be remiss if I did not conduct a complete oral history with this man who had had so much to do with the history of the Disney organization. So, on November 5, 1975, Floyd and I sat down with my tape recorder, and the following interview is the result of that session.

S: Floyd, my first question is why did you come to work at the Disney Studio, and who was your first contact?

G: Well, I had been doing cartoon work back in Utah for four or five years. I was studying by correspondence through the Federal Schools at that time. We lived 180 miles south of Salt Lake City, and there were no art schools in the area—these were "horse and buggy" days—so this was the only way to study. Earlier I had completed a couple of

Gottfredson felt that Goofy—known initially as Dippy Dawg—was "the best comic foil of all the secondary characters." His appearance in the strip was Gottfredson's effort "to emulate what they were doing in the films."

courses with the Landon Schools in Cleveland, but this course with the Federal Schools was more extensive. One thing I did through the school was to enter a national cartoon contest that was sponsored by the American Tree Association. Several top-notch editorial cartoonists, like Jay and Darling, were to judge us. I won second place.

S: Why did you decide to come to Los Angeles?

G: Los Angeles had more opportunity, with seven newspapers at that time, between Los Angeles and Hollywood, but I couldn't get a job on any of them. I had worked as a movie projectionist in a small theater chain back in Utah, so I went back to work as a projectionist. Remember, this was still in the silent days; we were just converting to sound. I was working

98

the theater downtown on Main Street called the Third Street Theater—it was named the Third Street Theater because Third Street ran to this theater and stopped. After I'd been there about six months, the city decided to extend the street and they tore down the theater—I was out of work again! One day in December 1929, I was down on what they then called "Film Row"—where all of the film distributors had their offices—on Vermont Avenue. I was browsing

around, trying to get another job as a projectionist when I happened to notice the exchange that was distributing the **Mickey Mouse** films. They had a one-sheet board propped out in front, and a couple of posters in the window. So, I just walked in and started talking to a guy, and we got around to the fact that I, as a projectionist back in Utah, had run all the **Oswald** films but none of the **Mickeys**. I hadn't seen any of them yet, so I was interested in them. In the

course of talking to this guy, he said, "Look, I heard Walt is going back to New York looking for artists next week. Why don't you go out there?" So, I did. Of course, I had no idea that it was animators that he was looking for, but I bundled up my samples and went out to the Studio. Walt looked at them and he said, "Yes, we'll put you to work in animation here." When he asked me what sort of work I was interested in, I replied, "I'm actually more interested in comic strip work than I am in animation." It just happened that they were developing the **Mickey Mouse** daily comic strip then. They had been working on it for about six months—Walt, Ub Iwerks, and Win Smith. Walt said, "Well, you don't want to get involved in that. Comic strip work is a rat race, and there's no future in it. Animation is where the future's going to be." So I said, "Fine, I'll try it then." And I was hired as an inbetweener.

S: How much were you paid?

G: Actually I had been working as a projectionist for $65 a week, which was good money in the late 1920s. At Disney, I started at $18 a week. That was the scale; you got that or else. They just didn't pay beginners any more than that. So this was something of a problem—I was married, and had a couple of children. But I decided that this was what I was looking for, and so I'd better try to work it out some way. I worked four months in animation as an inbetweener, doing inbetweens for Johnny Cannon, and later for Dave Hand and Wilfred Jackson, and maybe a dozen inbetweens for Ub Iwerks one time.

S: Do you recall what films you worked on?

G: They were all **Silly Symphonys**.[1] "Summer"

[1] *The* Silly Symphony *cartoon shorts and the early Sunday comic strips both call for a* Silly Symphonys *plural. In later years the comic strip was renamed* Silly Symphonies, *though the films were not.*

Mickey Mouse's first appearance in daily newspapers was on January 13, 1930—a strip written by Walt Disney, penciled by Disney's chief animator Ub Iwerks, and inked by Win Smith. The first panel is reproduced here the size it was drawn.

Many *Mickey Mouse* gags that were acceptable in the early 1930s, such as having a piece of Mickey's tail snipped off, were toned down in later years.

was one of them, and "Autumn," and then there was a jungle **Silly Symphony** of some kind. I think it was "Cannibal Capers." The reason I remember it was because Norm Ferguson (Fergy, to us) was doing that, and he and Dave Hand gave me a little piece of animation to do by myself. That was the only actual animation I did. I did a little 24-drawing cycle of a cannibal beating a drum for Dave Hand. Then Fergy did about four extremes of a lion running out of the jungle way in the background and up past the camera. He said, "Take this and animate it." I replied that I didn't know anything about animating, but he said, "You've been around long enough and you've worked on enough of these things that you know the general principles. See what you can do with it." So I did do it, and it worked out. These were the only two things I ever did.

S: How long did you remain an inbetweener?

G: I was in inbetweens about four months. I was getting quite interested and fascinated with it. Meanwhile, Win Smith was working on the comic strip getting it ready to go to the Syndicate. King Features had come to Walt—after Mickey's big success in the theaters—and asked him to do the **Mickey** strip. Walt wrote the first eighteen gags—these were adaptations of gags that were lifted from the films—and Ub penciled them and Win Smith inked them. After that, Walt continued writing the strip, first with little continuities that ran about a week, but they were all based on gags that were lifted from the pictures. When Ub left the Studio, Win then penciled and inked the strip. After about three and

a half months, King Features requested that Walt expand the continuities and get away from the daily gag business. **The Gumps** had really pioneered the continuities, and that strip became so popular, all the syndicates pushed their artists to try continuities. The old "gag-a-day" situations slowly disappeared. Walt, in the meantime, had been trying to get Win to take over the writing as well as the drawing. I don't know why Win was stalling—perhaps he felt that he couldn't do it, or he didn't want the extra work. He was sort of a strange character anyway. He had a big brass spittoon in the corner of his room, about two feet high, and he had tobacco juice about a foot and a half above the spittoon. He was ambidextrous—he drew with his right hand and wrote with his left hand. He described himself as "a boy from the toolies," which was a little odd because I was 24 at the time, Walt was 28, and Win was about 43. We thought of him as an old man.

S: Had he done comic strip work before?

G: I don't think he had done actual comic strip work, but he had done newspaper cartoon work for several years. Finally, Walt called Win in for a showdown on this writing thing, and I guess they had a big blowup in his office because Win came storming out to my desk and he said, "I guess you got a new job." I asked him why, and he said, "Well, I've quit." And I said, "Why, for hell's sake?" He said, "No goddamn young whippersnapper's gonna tell me what to do." So he walked out of the Studio into oblivion, and, of course, the young whippersnapper became

world-renowned.

S: Did you ever hear from Win Smith again?

G: We did, I would say in about 1942 or 1944—I'm just guessing at the time. Joe Reddy in Publicity got a letter from his widow, and she said he had been teaching cartooning in connection with a high school down in Phoenix, Arizona, and he had passed away just recently. She wanted to know if the Studio wanted his drawing board, because she said this was the one **Mickey Mouse** was started on. Joe came to me, and I said, "Well, that must be the one that he used at home, because I'm still working on the one that he started on at the Studio." I remembered that Win had brought his board into the Studio, and when he left, the Studio bought it from him, and I inherited it when I went onto the job. I guess when Win brought his into the Studio he bought himself another one for home, because he was doing work both at home and in the Studio at the time. Anyway, we thanked Mrs. Smith but declined her offer.

S: How did you happen to take over the strip?

G: Walt called me in after Win quit and asked me to take the strip over. I reminded him of what he had told me when I came in, and I added, "You were right. I've become interested in animation now, and I'd rather stay with it." He said, "Well, Floyd, take it over for a couple of weeks, while I find someone." And this two weeks, of course, dragged into a month, and I began to wonder if he was looking for anyone. And then, after a couple of months, I began to worry for fear that he **was,** that he might find someone—because I now had regained my old interest in comic strips. And the subject was never brought up again. Forty-six years later I was still doing the strip—until I retired.

S: Floyd, could we digress a little so you could tell me a little bit about the Disney Studio at that time—what the facilities were like, how many rooms there were, where the comic strips were done, and so forth.

G: When I came to Disney, the Studio had been located on Hyperion Avenue for about four years. But there was only the small front building. The distinctive main animation building with its elaborate neon-lit sign advertising Mickey Mouse would not come for several years. In the building, there was a row of front offices facing Hyperion. Roy's secretary, Lucille Benedict, had the first one. Walt's office was next to hers, and Roy's was behind that. Directly behind the entrance was a large room, divided by a ten-foot-high partition. On one side of the partition were all the animators; on the other side were the inkers and painters, and behind them was the camera with two operators. When I came, Bill Cottrell and Chuck Couch were operating the camera. Hazel Sewell was in charge of Ink and Paint. Directly behind Walt's office was the Music Room, occupied by Carl Stalling. This was also the gag conference room where once a week, after work, all the animators were expected to stay over for a gag meeting. It usually ran from about 8 to 10 o'clock.

S: Did you attend these meetings?

G: Yes, I attended a couple of them. I remember one night—I think it was the second gag meeting I attended—Walt came up to me. He knew that I lived way out in West Los Angeles, and I had no car. I had to catch a bus from the Hyperion Studio to Sanborn Junction, which was the corner of Sanborn and Santa Monica Blvd., and then catch the red cars and ride those home. It took about an hour and a half each way to travel. Walt knew this, and he also knew that after 10 o'clock, when the gag meeting was over, there were no buses running in front of the Studio. The first time I had stayed for a gag meeting, I had

to walk to Sanborn Junction, about a mile and a half. So, after this second meeting, Walt said, "Stick around a little while, until I clean up a few things, and I'll drive you home." And I said, "Gee whiz, Walt, you don't need to do that. It's 25 miles out there." (At that time the Studio and Walt and Roy owned one car—it was a little

A 1936 or '37 photo of Gottfredson "working" on a Donald Duck *Silly Symphony*. There's no record that Gottfredson ever drew the strip, but he may have "helped out" at times.

black Ford runabout with one seat in it and a little pickup truck thing behind.) But Walt said, "No, I'll enjoy taking you out there. I sometimes like to drive around awhile alone, to think and work out some problems. I'll do that on the way back." So he drove me home that night and we had a nice visit.

S: I understand Ub Iwerks was the top animator.

G: That's right. He was doing most of his own inbetweens and still was faster than anyone else. I would say that Ub was turning out twice or three times as much animation as any other animator in the Studio. He was considered the top animator in the world by everybody in the business—principally because of the rubbery, loose action that he developed in the **Oswald** pictures and then brought to a head with "The Skeleton Dance," which began the **Silly Symphonys.** Ub was very quiet; he just sat there and worked all day long. But he also did all the storyboards or story sketches on all the pictures. He did a lot of the posters—even that late he was doing an occasional poster or publicity drawing. When Walt had his break with his distributor, Pat Powers, Ub was courted by Powers who offered to set him up in his own studio. It was really an offer that Ub could not refuse, so when he left the Studio, he tried to get two or three of Walt's animators to go with him—I suppose Wilfred Jackson and maybe Les Clark—but he only was able to get Ham Hamilton, who had left Walt some time earlier to go over to Universal. It was at this time that I did the half a dozen or so inbetweens for Ub. One day he turned around and handed these to me and said, "Do these for me, will ya?" And I couldn't believe it: here was the great Ub Iwerks asking me to do inbetweens! So I flipped through the things, and down in the middle of them was a note asking me to meet him for lunch. So, I went off with him and he told me that he'd been watching me and he was impressed with my work and would like to have me come to work for him. This was the first I knew he was setting up his own studio. I was quite flattered.

S: Did he offer you more money?

G: Yes, he offered me $25 a week—and this, of course, was an inducement, too. So, I said, "Well, sure." I was quite sure that I wasn't important enough to Walt and Roy for them to miss me—after all I had only been at the Studio for less than a month—and this looked like a good opportunity for me to step up. I knew by then that Ub was **the** man in the animation business, and he told me that he would be able to teach me a lot of things that would be beneficial to me.

So it was quite an attractive offer. I signed a contract with Ub, but then I got to worrying about it, and I talked to Jackson, and I talked to Bert Gillett, and they both said, "No, you're absolutely wrong about Ub, and you shouldn't have done this. While Ub is a great animator, Walt is really the brains and the creative man here—he's the man who's going to build this place into something really big. We doubt that Ub has the business ability to make a go of his studio." It was approaching time for me to leave, and so I went to Roy and laid all the cards on the table. Roy turned red in the face and he picked up his phone and called Ub. He said, "Look, Ub, this Gottfredson thing is the last straw. You've been trying to get our key men around here, trying to get anybody that you can, while Walt's back in New York looking for animators. We've just had enough of this, and it's got to stop." And he said, "We're not going to let Gottfredson go." Needless to say, this surprised me.

S: Obviously you didn't realize how indispensable you were.

G: Yeah; how about that! Roy really ripped into Ub over the phone and Ub told Roy, "Well, it's not that important to me. If Floyd wants to stay with you, just tell him to tear up the contract and that will be the end of it." So Roy said, "Well, that's the way it's going to be," and he slammed down the phone. Then he turned around to me and told me about it, and I said, "Frankly, Roy, this is a big relief to me, because I've been talking to some of the guys and gotten myself straightened out and I realized I made a mistake. I'm very happy it's turned out this way. I am sorry if I've caused any trouble between you and Ub."

S: He didn't give you a raise on the spot?

G: No. In fact he said, "Look, you're not that important to us; don't get that idea. This thing had just gone far enough with Ub; we were just putting a stop to it." So that is how I came to stay at the Disney Studio. As I had been warned,

Ub's studio didn't last more than three or four years, and I guess Ub was out of work for several years. It was about ten years before Walt finally brought him back here, which I thought was another good example of how big Walt really was. The whole relationship between him and Ub was very deep, and he recognized Ub's genius, too. So it was a very sensible and profitable thing for both Walt and Ub when he called him back to the Studio.

S: Getting back to the arrangement of the building—you didn't mention where the comic strips were drawn.

G: Ub and [Wilfred] Jackson sat right behind me. With our backs to them, there was Johnny Cannon near the walkway, then my desk, and then Dave Hand's. On toward the back of the building there was a little cubbyhole that must not have been over seven-by-eight feet, something like that, and that's where Win Smith worked with the comic strip. There was no outside light in there, just an overhead light hanging down, and then his desk lamp on his board. When Win walked out, I had moved into his cubbyhole, and I worked there, I guess, for two, maybe three months before this addition was finished. In 1931, some time after Carl Stalling had left the Studio, Comic Strip was moved into the old Music Room. It was at this time that Al Taliaferro joined the department—he was the second one in the department after me. Before that time, I had had some occasional inking assistants, and one writer assistant. Walt, attempting to gag the continuities up and make them funnier, hired a gag writer from Screen Gems at Columbia, whose name I cannot recall. I would write the continuities and take them over to him, and he'd go over and write gags on them and bring them back to me. I'd then go over his stuff and edit

it, because it was so wordy. He was only there temporarily, only a couple of months. He later committed suicide in Hollywood.

S: Who else was working for the Comic Strip Department at that time?

G: Earl Duvall came in and did my inking for a while. He also drew a couple of weeks of **Mickeys**, but then he went into Story. Roy Nelson, who was a cartoonist from a Chicago paper, was out doing a tour of Hollywood studios. When he came by Disney's, Walt put him to work on publicity drawings for the Studio, and also had him help me with the inking. He was there for a couple of months. Then Hardie Gramatky came in, working on publicity drawings and inking my dailies. Hardie was only with me for a few months, and then he went into animation. When he moved into the Music Room, Al Taliaferro came on then as a regular, to work directly on the comic strip as my inker.

S: What can you tell me about Al Taliaferro?

G: Al came to the Studio in '31, as I said, to ink my stuff on the strip. He had worked as a lighting fixture designer, and that was the only professional job he had had up until then. He had taken the Federal Schools cartooning course, and finished that. He was a friend of Wilfred Jackson, and Jackson was aware of what he'd been doing and what he wanted to do, so Jackson brought him into the Studio. We were looking for someone to ink my material, so that's why he was brought in. He did publicity drawings and inked my strips until we started the **Silly Symphony** section in 1933. This was the time I started the **Mickey** Sunday page—King Features had been after Walt for I guess nearly a year to do a Sunday page. Walt had thus been after me to do it, and I couldn't find the time. Finally the pressure got so great, and because I now had Al inking my material and Ted Osborne doing the writing, I was able to get into the Sunday page. But to get it started, Earl Duvall, who was still with the Story Department, did the first **Mickey** Sunday page. And then I took it from there. Now in those days, a Sunday page was comprised of two subjects. It took up a full page in the newspaper, but one half of the page was the main subject, which was a **Mickey Mouse** in our case, and the top half was a **Silly Symphony**. Earl Duvall wrote and drew, penciled and inked the **Silly Symphonys**. The **Silly Symphonys** were done in verse, to help catch the flavor of the pictures themselves. In early 1933, Al Taliaferro took over the **Silly Symphonys**. Duvall then went to the Story Department full time, and besides the **Silly Symphony** work, Al continued to ink my dailies and Sundays too. In the meantime, we had added Tom Wood, who came into the department as a publicity artist, and also to do the lettering on all the comic strips. Tom worked in that capacity for about a year and a half, until the publicity work grew to a point where he needed to develop his own department.

S: Who replaced Tom Wood in your area?

G: We brought in Ted Thwaites then. Ted had been working on the **Examiner** downtown, and he was a fellow who Charlie Philippi, one of the layout artists, and Tom Wood knew. They had him come in and we had him take over the inking and lettering of the **Mickey** dailies and Sundays, while Al continued to draw, ink and letter the **Silly Symphonys**. Al would also do an occasional Sunday page for me, when things got too hectic, because the department was slowly building now. Things continued this way until about

1937. Al had been dying to get his own strip all during this time. Al was a pretty ambitious guy, hard working and a fast worker, too. So, by this time Donald Duck had been introduced in the pictures, and Al thought he could be a great character for him to develop into his own strip. He went to Roy, and Roy wasn't really interested in it. He said, "There's no use getting into the complications of something else." But Al kept pestering him, until finally Roy said, "Well, all right. Do up two or three weeks of them and we'll send them to the Syndicate and see if they are interested." So, Al did his own gags for the first three weeks, and he drew them up and inked them and sent them to the Syndicate, and the Syndicate rejected them. By this time, Merrill de Maris had joined the Comic Strip Department as a writer—he had replaced Ted Osborne. Merrill did three weeks on the **Duck** daily. Al drew those up and sent them back and the Syndicate again turned them down. So then Bob Karp, who was working in the Character Model Department, heard that we were having trouble doing gags for **Donald Duck**. He submitted two or three weeks of gags in his rough form. They looked good to me. Al drew those up and we sent them back to the Syndicate and the Syndicate bought them.

S: Wasn't Donald Duck introduced first to the comic strips in the **Silly Symphonys**?

G: That's right. In August 1936, Ted Osborne and Al Taliaferro did a brief feature with the Duck.[2] We had been doing adaptations of the actual **Silly Symphonys**, as long as they lasted.

But as the series started dwindling off and eventually quit, we ran out of subjects to do. So, we began to introduce things—like we did a equence for a while with Pluto, and a sequence with Donald Duck, and so on, to carry the section on. So, Al went on and developed Donald into the daily, with Bob Karp writing it. Then in 1939, Al and Bob, who were both quite ambitious types, agitated to get a Sunday page. Again, Roy was not very interested in the Sunday page, but Bob and Al kept hammering at him, and finally they offered to do the Sunday page for no extra money until they could get the thing established. Roy accepted this, and Al and Bob got the thing started.

S: Were you paid by the strip for each one that you turned out?

G: No, we were paid salaries. Everybody in the department was paid salaries, and we were just expected to maintain the schedule. As it has always been, and still is, we got no vacations as such. If we wanted a vacation, we just had to get the schedule two weeks or whatever ahead, and then take our vacation. If we didn't do that, we didn't get it. This was understood—it was just the way the comic strip business worked in the

[2] *For clarification, Donald Duck was introduced to comic strips in the* Silly Symphony *Sunday on September 16, 1934 in an adaptation of "The Wise Little Hen." From August 30, 1936 through December 5, 1937 Donald took over the* Silly Symphony *feature. Donald first appeared in the* Mickey Mouse *Sundays on February 10, 1935 and in the* Mickey *daily strip on March 14, 1935.*

Gottfredson often commented that Disney occasionally received complaints "from the P.T.A. and organizations of that kind" when he depicted a cow's udders in his cartoon shorts or books.

whole newspaper industry. It has always been this way; it was never really an assignment deal or a piecework deal. It was always on salary, with full fringe benefits, as those fringe benefits developed in the Studio. In fact, Al Taliaferro was one of the few of us who got vacations, because he was able to turn out the work fast enough. (Al did a fine job with the **Donald** strip—hard worker, maintained schedules—until his illnesses struck him; he had a recurring cancer thing that bothered him off and on for 15 years before he died.) The salaries were never as high as those in animation until the union got into the thing, and then I think the scale for Class I Comic Strip Artist became the same as a minimum scale for an animator.

S: How did the Comic Strip Department evolve? And did you head it because you were the only one there to start with?

G: Yes, and this is how it grew. It was a one-man department at first and then, as the need arose through the years, I just added men. I meant to tell you about Osborne and de Maris. Ted Osborne and Dick Creedon were writers on a comedy-variety radio show that ran on KHJ— and I believe it was a daily thing, so it was a lot of work to write and produce. Walt brought the two fellows out from this radio show to develop a **Mickey Mouse** radio show. They produced some shows, but it didn't last very long. When the radio show failed, Walt had to find something else for Ted and Dick to do. So, he gave me Ted Osborne to write the comic strip material, and Dick Creedon went into Publicity. Publicity had by then developed into a three- or four-man art department under Tom Wood, and they had one publicity writer. Ted Osborne was my first

In 1929 the Studio, Walt, and Roy owned one car—a little black Ford runabout. When Gottfredson attended a late gag meeting, Walt personally drove him 25 miles to his home, explaining, "I'll enjoy taking you out there. I sometimes like to drive around awhile alone, to think and work out some problems. I'll do that on the way back." This 1931 photo with Walt is of the Studio's car the following year, when the company acquired a sedan.

regular writer. I had written everything up to that point. This was now in 1933, I think. So from that time on, Ted and I worked together. I plotted the continuities because I was used to them. For some strange reason all of the writers I ever had through the years up to Bill Walsh were clever writers, but they couldn't plot. These fellows were good at dialog, and especially good at puns, and puns were used quite extensively in comic strips then, and they were good enough at it that they've been mentioned several times in the anthologies about comics, but for some reason they just had no aptitude for plotting continuities. So, I continued plotting the things, and the way we would work—I would work up the

general plot, the story line, for the continuities, and then we would sit down and talk out what we planned to do for the coming week. We'd pretty well work out all the business, and generally the dialog, and then the writer would take this and break it down into strips and write it up on the typewriter. I'd go over that and edit it, and then I'd draw the things. So Merrill de Maris at that time was in the Story Department, so he traded them. He took Osborne up to Story and sent de Maris down to me. After three or four months, something like that, he became unhappy with Osborne in Story, and was now becoming impressed with what de Maris was doing on the comic strips, so he traded again.

I was never consulted on these things. Walt would just call and inform me that he was making the switch.

S: Perhaps these guys were both good at comic strip but neither of them was good at animation story.

G: Yes, well, it was not only that, but I guess the bull sessions that we were having, and the fact that I was directing the general line of the continuities was the thing that made them hang together. Comic strip historians have asked me why with the three or four writers I had over the years, the general flavor and spirit of the continuities remained the same, and why the personalities of the writers weren't

In early December of 1929 while browsing on Vermont Avenue's "Film Row," Gottfredson spotted his first *Mickey Mouse* cartoon one sheet. What he saw was probably either the stock one sheet, "Here Today," or a poster of the newly released "Haunted House."

Scene 7 - BACKGD A   Hunted

When asked if the animators drew from or were influenced by his daily strip, Gottfredson joked that "they didn't know we existed!" He admitted, in fact, that "it was the other way around. I was trying my best to catch the spirit of the animation." Many of the first four months' gags and portions of the first continuity, "Mickey Mouse in Death Valley" (right), were written by Walt himself and set the precedent for "borrowing" from the cartoons.

reflected in the stories that they wrote. I guess the answer is that I plotted all of them through the years, and I edited everything, and we had bull sessions and talked over the business. Well, this was what was happening to Osborne and de Maris. Working as we did down there, they were turning out good work. But Walt thought that they were doing everything—the plotting, the editing, and everything else. Finally, in late '37 or early '38, Walt made the last change and sent de Maris back to me and took Osborne back into Story. After everything mushroomed after **Snow White**, all the departments like ours on the fringe of the Studio were pushed out into outlying sections. We went to the second floor of the Ontra Cafeteria over in Hollywood, on Vine Street just off Hollywood Blvd. Some of the Story Department staff went down to Seward Street, and that was where Ted Osborne went, to work on **Bambi**. When the Seward Street Story Department folded prior to the move to Burbank, Osborne, because he had been the original writer, came to me and wanted to come back to this department. This meant that I would have to let de Maris go. There was no place for him to go then—and of the two writers, de Maris was the better. De Maris was a very talented writer, but Osborne was sort of mechanical. He had a tremendous gag file, but he did everything by formula. So, I had to make a decision, and decided to keep de Maris. Osborne left the Studio then, and de Maris stayed with me until '42. When de Maris left, Bob Karp, who had been wanting to get more things to do, wanted to take over the **Mickey** writing. I talked to Vern Caldwell, who was then the liaison man between Roy Disney and me, and he said, "Sure, give him a try." So, Bob worked, I think, on maybe two weeks of the **Mickey** daily and Sunday, and Roy Disney got word of it. Roy had been down on the Karp family because, in his opinion, we had too many of them here, and they were trying to pull in more all the time. I don't know whether Bob Karp or Lynn Karp came first; Lynn was in animation. Then in '39, Bob got his brother Hubie in to take over some gag writing for the films, and then later when de Maris left the Studio, Bob had Hubie writing the **Silly Symphonys**. In the meantime, they were trying to get their dad in the Studio. So, when Roy heard that Bob was going to take over the **Mickey** daily and Sunday writing after de Maris left, Roy said, "No, we've got too many of those Karps in there now, and I just don't want to be that dependent on Bob writing so many

Disney features. You'll have to get someone else." So, Dick Shaw came in and wrote continuities for awhile, but Dick was a gag man and an animation story man, and he couldn't handle continuities. I didn't have the time to spend with him to work out the plots so we were looking for a new man, a good writer. Hal Adelquist at that time was sort of a personnel director for Walt—I don't know exactly what his duties or his title were—but it was something to that effect anyway. Vern Caldwell had gone to Hal and told him that we were looking for a writer and we needed one pretty badly. Hal called me and said, "I'm going to send down a **Liberty Magazine** that has an article supposedly written by Gracie Allen in it." So I read it, and he said, "Now you

probably wouldn't know that this thing was ghostwritten for her." And I replied, "Yes, I assumed so, but, I'll tell you this—whoever did it sure did a great job. It sounds exactly as if Gracie had written it herself." Hal said, "If you had a chance to hire that fellow as your writer, would you take him?" And I said, "In a minute!" This turned out to be Bill Walsh. It developed that Bill was part owner of the Margaret Ettinger Advertising Agency in Hollywood, and he'd been working as a gag writer and public relations man for Burns and Allen, and also for Bergen and McCarthy. He was also a friend of Vern Caldwell's, and Vern had been trying to get him out here for quite a while as a publicity writer, but Bill was so big that the Studio couldn't afford

to pay him what he had to have in order to join the staff. So Vern had talked to Hal, and said, "If Floyd could use him on the comic strips, then between the two jobs we could afford him." So, I told Vern that I would like to give him a try, and Bill joined the staff. I worked with Bill for the first two or three months quite closely. I had to practically rewrite everything that he did at first because he was so production-minded that it would have taken four strips to draw what he wrote for one strip. It was this sort of a thing with him. But all the talent and ability were there; it was just a matter of working him into the process of learning the limitations of writing for comic strips. Of course, he eventually learned this very quickly. He was such a talented guy.

S: Wasn't it getting a little hectic for you running the Comic Strip Department?

G: Yes, but things were changing. We now had seven features in the department, and we had about four writers and five artists. I was trying to run the department and still pencil the **Mickey** dailies. Manuel Gonzales had taken over the penciling of the **Mickey** Sunday in 1938. We had Ted Thwaites inking, and Bill Wright had come into the department, working as Ted's assistant, inking. So by now, trying to manage the department and continue drawing and editing everything was getting to be too much for me. So I had talks with Vern Caldwell, and Vern talked to Ward Greene at King Features, and they decided that what the Studio needed was to get someone who could work full time as a comic strip editor and manage the department, as well as take over some of Roy Disney's comic strip chores which necessitated occasional trips to New York. They first asked me to give up the drawing and take over the job, and I thought it over, but I decided no—that I was primarily an artist and I just wouldn't be happy in that sort

Frank Reilly, a former Associated Press comics editor, took over as Editor/Manager/Administrator of the Comic Strip Department after WWII. Shown with Gottfredson in this 1967 Studio photo, it was Reilly who decided in the 1950s that Mickey should become a "suburbanite family man."

of work. I didn't enjoy editing and tearing other people's work apart, and having to cope with personalities and all those things. I decided that I would rather carry on as the **Mickey Mouse** artist. Frank Reilly, who had been a comics editor for Associated Press Syndicate in New York, was just getting out of the army after World War II. He was a friend of Ward Greene's and Ward suggested that the Studio offer the job to Frank. So that is how Frank came into the Studio as the editor/manager/administrator of the Comic Strip Department. I became his assistant, and operated that way, when he would use me, through the years.

S: Were there the equivalent of gag meetings that you people had for the comic strips, or was it pretty much up to the writer to come up with his own idea?

G: Well, as I said before, I plotted the very general story line for the continuities. And then the writer and I would have bull sessions, which amounted to gag meetings. We'd sit down and talk over everything we were going to do in the coming week, and break it down. We would break it down strip by strip. Then the writer would take it and break it down panel by panel and write it up into strips with the complete dialog and give it to me, and I'd go over it and edit it. I worked that way with Bill Walsh for probably the first two months. Then, he took over the writing and the plotting on his own, and all I did was edit as he'd bring these things in. We just couldn't get him to pare the dialog and the business in the strips down to the comic strip's limitations, so I said, "Look—write every-

thing you want into them. We would much rather have more things than we can use than not enough. You give them to me and I'll pare them down to the comic strip format, so that they'll work in there." So this is the way we worked together. Gonzy—Gonzales—especially would get so exasperated. I wouldn't attempt to cut out the description and the business with the props so much as I would the dialog when I edited them. Then I would just draw in what I felt was the best of the props and the business that he suggested, and leave the rest out. But Gonzy had a problem with this because he wanted to draw everything in, and he couldn't. There was too much work, and he beefed about Bill writing so much stuff into it all the time to a point where we began to refer to Bill as "Cecil B. de Walsh." Anyway, that's the way we worked with Bill until, of course, he gradually attracted Walt's attention with his publicity writing to a point where Walt made him a producer. Bill hung on to the writing of the comic strips way beyond what he should as far as his time limitations were concerned. He just enjoyed doing it; he didn't want to give it up. Frank finally had to just practically force him to, because he was getting to a point where I would have to run over to Bill's office and pick up the **Mickey** daily script one strip at a time. Of course, that just wasn't practical. Finally he left, and Frank then put Roy Williams on writing the **Mickey** dailies. This went on for about three or four years, but then we began to get complaints from the Syndicate because Roy's writing was too childish. There wasn't much we could do about it. Frank did a lot of editing on his stuff. Roy was the kind of

a guy—and he was the same way in Story, too, and anyone who worked with him will tell you the same thing—he cranked out gags just like he was literally cranking a machine, but he couldn't tell the good ones from the bad ones. And he admitted it. It got to a point where he was submitting four or five weeks of **Mickey** dailies for one week that we would get out of them. Then Frank would tell him, "Look, can't you be a little more discriminating about these things? You could save yourself an awful lot of work if, after you've got several of these written, you'd go through them and throw out the bad ones. That would save me work, too." Roy threw up his hands and said, "I can't do that. I can't tell the good ones from the bad ones. If I had to do that, I'd have to quit."

S: Did Walt take much of an interest in the comic strip as it was going along? Did you get criticism or story suggestions from him?

G: At the start I did. He would make suggestions every once in a while, for some short continuities and so on, and I would do them. One that I'll never forget, and which I still don't understand— around early 1931 I believe it was, he said, "Why don't you do a continuity of Mickey trying to commit suicide?" So I said, "Walt! You're kidding!" He replied, "No, I'm not kidding. I think you could get a lot of funny stuff out of that." I said, "Gee whiz, Walt, I don't know. What do you think the Syndicate will think of it? What do you think the editors will think? And the readers?" He said, "I think it will be funny. Go ahead and do it." So I did, oh, maybe ten days of Mickey trying to commit suicide—jumping off

Gottfredson felt that the major change in the strip over the years was "the new eye with the pupil in it, which came into being in 1938" in the Robinson Crusoe adventure (beginning with the December 22 daily), following the lead of the animated films.

Gottfredson and writer Bill Walsh decided in the mid-1940s that Mickey's two nephews, who looked exactly alike and had the same personality, were being duplicated too much in the *Donald Duck* strip by Huey, Dewey, and Louie. Gottfredson's solution was to "let Ferdie fade out of the picture so we could develop Morty as a little mechanical genius type."

bridges and landing in garbage scows, trying to hang himself and the limb breaks, rigging up a gun and something happens to it. I don't remember all the details. But, strangely enough, the Syndicate didn't object. We didn't hear anything from the editors, and Walt said, "See, it was funny; I told you it would be." So, there were a few things like that.

S: Did you have much in the way of censorship problems from the Syndicate or anyone else?

G: Well, there was the incident about the "Monarch of Medioka," which people recognized as Yugoslavia. Through the years we have had to change things, and it still happens occasionally now, things that they think might be a little off-color or might be mistaken for a sex symbol, or some such thing as this. Or it might be anything that might mislead children, some sort of gag they might try to emulate and hurt themselves. This goes on all the time. I know that we had a situation where we had one of the characters, I think it was Donald Duck, answering the phone in the bathtub. We got a question on that, and Frank went to the phone company here and got a very lengthy explanation to the effect that it wasn't dangerous. While they didn't recommend it, it wasn't dangerous. So that strip got through. But, through the years, there weren't too many of these. I think Walt ran up against more things from the P.T.A. and organizations of that kind with his cartoon shorts. I think this was one of the things that led him to change Mickey from the dashing little daredevil

character to the domesticated mouse.

S: How did Mickey change in the strip over the years?

G: During the continuities—this is the way Walt started him out in the continuity and it's the way I carried him on—he was a Mouse Against The World sort of character. Not that he was belligerent or militant, or really **against** the world—it was just that the world was so much bigger than him. He was constantly getting into scrapes and situations that he had to fumble his way out of—not as dangerous as Superman or anything—but in a funny sort of way. When he was in a corner, he was a feisty little guy, who would fight his way out—pretty scrappy and so on. He remained pretty much that way all through the continuities. But when we stopped the continuities and got into the gag-a-day business, Frank Reilly then decided that the strip should become a suburban, sort of family neighborhood kind of thing. This was when Mickey did a complete about-face, as far as I am concerned, in the strip, and I'm sure most of the readers and fans agreed, too, that he became just a straight man for the guys who could do the gags better, such as Goofy and Morty and Pluto and Minnie and Clarabelle, and characters of this kind. He just since that time has been a sort of ineffectual little straight man, just another suburbanite family man, as so many of the other suburban strips are. This was the thing that I was never happy about, myself, but it was a decision that was the way Frank saw him, and apparently the

Syndicate agreed with him. It would be nice if we could bring back Mickey's personality, with its foibles and idiosyncrasies, so that he could handle comedy again.

S: What have been the physical changes that have taken place in Mickey over the years?

G: I would say that the major change was, of course, the new eye with the pupil in it, which came into being in 1938; I understand there's still a little controversy as to whether Fred Moore or Ward Kimball did the first one. Fred Moore, I'm sure, had more to do with developing it than anybody else, and very likely used it first in the shorts. As far as his appearance—the clothing, dropping the short pants and so on—we have always felt that that wasn't too great a change in that Mickey has always been an actor in the films, so he adopted the costume of whatever part he was playing at the time, whether he was a bandmaster, or a fireman, or a brave little tailor, or the Sorcerer's Apprentice, or whatever. As time went on and as they began to put him in suits and long pants in the pictures, we just went along. We never initiated anything like that in the strips. Basically, I've always felt that it was our job to try to catch the spirit of animation and bring what they were doing in animation to the strip. This is what I tried to do in my design and in the action; I tried to make the characters move and design them as if they were moving in animation. Then as our continuities went along, and it became more desirable to put Mickey in a costume that fit the continuity, we just gradually evolved the short-sleeved shirt and the long pants and occasionally the hat that he now wears in the strip.

S: What about his tail?

G: The tail was dropped briefly during the war. As I understand this, it was because of the limited number of animation personnel here. They felt that it just would save some time in animation. The tail was a thing that always had to be drawn to move pretty gracefully, so it required a little attention. Thus, Walt had them drop it during the war, when the animation staff was so cut back. Then, after the war, when they decided to bring it back on again, Walt asked Frank to reinstate the tail on Mickey, and we've had it with us ever since. I don't know whether anyone ever noticed, but as far as I know, we've never had any fan mail or comments on it.

S: Were there any times when something originated in the **Mickey Mouse** comic strip rather than in the films?

G: I don't think so. Certainly nothing that we ever adopted in the films. Whether Fred Moore was influenced by what we had been doing with Mickey's costume in the strip when he designed the clothing for "Plight of the Bumble Bee," a picture that was never finished or released, I don't know. He did the model sheet on it, and Mickey was pretty well dressed the same as we

had carried him in the strip. The only thing that I know in the Comic Strip Department that was adopted in the pictures was Al's creation of Donald's nephews in the **Donald Duck** daily strip. Al's widow, Lucy, called me recently to read me a memo she had found while cleaning up Al's stuff at home. It was from someone in the Story Department, thanking Al for having created the nephews and telling him that they were going to use them in a short and since he created them, they not only wanted to go on record as acknowledging the fact that he had, but also wanted to recognize it with a check, which they had apparently sent him. None of the characters I created for the **Mickey** strip ever went into animation.

S: Where did Mickey's nephews come from?

G: I think Walt asked me to take a couple of the mice in the audience in "Orphan's Benefit" and make nephews out of them for Mickey, so I did and for the first several years in the strip they wore the little skirts and little sailor hats and had a little spiked tail. That spiked tail was Walt's idea to the animators—he said, "I think it would be funny if we had that little spiked tail sticking up so that the skirt could drape over it." Frank Reilly never liked that spiked tail. He tried to talk me out of it a time or two, and I had to keep reminding him that this was Walt's innovation, and his idea. Anyway, it was just another little

thing to distinguish Morty from Mickey. When Al introduced the Duck nephews, he did it emulating the three nephews in **Happy Hooligan** that Opper had done. Hooligan had three little nephews that were all identical, so Al said, "I think it would be funny for Donald to have three nephews." And I said, "You're cooking yourself up a lot of work." And he replied, "Well, I think it will be fun, and we can cut one of them out occasionally." We had introduced the Mickey nephews before Al had the comic strip but we didn't consider making a change in them until after Bill Walsh came in. We decided, to start with, that the two nephews who looked exactly alike and had exactly the same personality in the **Mickey** comic strip was being duplicated too much with the three nephews in the **Duck** strip, and we figured we ought to develop personalities with the **Mickey** nephews. So, Bill and I decided that we'd just let Ferdie fade out of the picture so we could develop Morty as a little mechanical genius type. We'd eventually give him the little notched cap that the mechanics wear, put a couple of buttons on it, and have him constantly working with mechanics and machines in the garage, fixing things all the time. We would develop him, then after a while bring Ferdie back into the picture and explain that he'd been away to school and he comes back a little bookworm. He would have the little Eton cap, and wear glasses, and the little Eton-type coat, and things

A 1963 awards presentation photo, with recipients holding their inscribed Duckster or Mousecar (pronounced *Mouse-ker*, to rhyme with Oscar) statuettes: Robert Karp (Duckster), Walt Disney, Floyd Gottfredson (Mousecar), Al Taliaferro (Duckster), Manuel Gonzales (Mousecar), and Roy O. Disney.

of this kind. So, we would have two definite personalities. In the meantime, before we brought him back, Frank Reilly came into the picture, and he didn't favor the idea of bringing Ferdie back very strong. He said, "This would probably be just a complication and it won't be very interesting. As long as he's faded out of the picture, why don't we just forget him and just have one nephew?" So that's what became of Ferdie. We haven't used him in the strip since, I would say, mid-1945, at least.

S: How did Peg-Leg Pete lose his peg leg?

G: Actually, this is second-hand, because the change came in animation. At the time, the animators were going through a phase where they were very conscious of mass and weight in the characters. And here was a great gimmick to work it on—Peg-Leg Pete's great weight on his peg leg. So they began to exaggerate and have fun with it to a point where they were making it appear painful. It was actually painful to some of the more sensitive in the audience. Whenever he took a step on that leg, they were aware of it, and they winced, and it took their mind off the story. So Walt, as I understand it, just said, "The hell with it. You've gone too far with this thing, and even if we do not make him limp any more, they're still going to think about it hurting him. Let's get rid of it." And so they just apparently gave him another leg. We, again trying to follow what they were doing in the pictures, went along with them. When they put the shoe on his foot, we put the shoe on his foot. We felt that we had to explain it a little bit, since we were using Pete a lot more than they were, so we did have a brief explanation to the fact that he'd gotten himself a new artificial leg with a shoe on it. Then we just forgot it. Later on, we began to phase Pete out of the comic strips because he had gotten to a point where he'd become a cliché—people just expected him to be the heavy in every continuity we did. Occasionally we felt it would be fun to bring him back as a kind of a shocker for a time or two. We had always regretted having to give up the peg leg, so after he'd been out for awhile, where we felt that the readers had sort of forgotten the fact that he didn't have his peg leg, when we brought

him back we brought him back with the peg leg.

S: Of all the characters that Mickey worked with, which was the easiest to write stories about—Pluto, Minnie, Goofy. . .?

G: Goofy. He's the best comic foil; he always has been and he still is. He wasn't in all of the continuities, but he was in many of them because he was such a good foil for Mickey—he was a

Mickey Mouse, at a 1982 dinner party with honoree Gottfredson.

good contrast. During the days when Peg-Leg Pete dominated the continuities so much, we didn't need Goofy, and Peg-Leg Pete was in the continuities before there was any Goofy. When he started out, of course, he was not Goofy, he was Dippy Dawg.

S: Did you name him for the comic strips?

G: No, he was referred to as Dippy Dawg on the first model sheets that were drawn of him. Charlie Philippi created the character, and that

was the name he gave him. So, when Walt asked us to do him in the comic strip, we introduced him as Dippy Dawg. As I remember it, it was probably ["Editor-in-Grief"]—where Mickey was publishing a newspaper called **The War Drum**—back in 1934 that we started using Dippy Dawg.[3] Walt didn't like the character to start with; he didn't like his appearance. They kept working, trying to work out another character, until Art Babbitt came up with Goofy in "Moving Day." This is the first that I am aware of. Goofy's actual character was developed, I think, more by the voice that Pinto Colvig gave him. Pinto saw him as what he called an "Oregon apple-knocker." This was the way Pinto referred to him all the time. I think it was a combination of what Pinto did with the voice (and in Story, as he did a lot of the early Goofy stories) and the way Babbitt visualized him pictorially. We just went along in the strip and tried to emulate what they were doing in the films.

S: What were some of your favorite characters that you created for the strip back in the continuity days?

G: Well, the Bat Bandit was one of them. He was a very strong character.

S: Did you create Chief O'Hara?

G: Yes. Well, he was pretty much of a cliché, of course. They were doing these things in pictures and everything else using the Irish cop. We just figured an Irish chief would be a good one. So we did him, complete with a long upper lip and at first some Irish brogue, though we dropped that a bit later on.

S: Did you ever do any work specifically for comic books, the **Mickey Mouse Magazine**, or hardcover books?

G: No, I didn't. In fact, when some of my stuff was adapted for the comic books by Western

---

[3] *Gottfredson's recollection of the first appearance of Dippy Dawg in the daily Mickey Mouse comic strip was confused with Donald Duck's March 14, 1935 debut in "Editor-in-Grief." Dippy had begun as a regular a year and a half earlier in October 1933. (see page 97). Both Donald and Dippy appeared in the Sunday pages before the dailies.*

Printing, they had to change the format so that the panels would fit in the magazines. Sometimes they'd have to crop off some of the drawing, and sometimes they'd have to add something to it—with the result that there are some pretty weird-looking hands and feet and things of this kind in the comic books through the years. For a long time, King Features was sending the originals directly to Western, and then Western would cut them up and reshape them and revamp the format, to fit the comic magazine and the comic books. That's why there are so few originals from the early days. Plus, around 1957, Frank had all of our originals prior to 1954 that were here at the Studio destroyed. They were piling up to a point where we were just running out of space to keep them, and the fire inspectors were complaining about their being a fire hazard. Of course, there was no Disney Archives then, and the collectors' fad hadn't come into being yet. Nobody could foresee that there was anything else to do with them.

S: Has it bothered you over the years that it was the **Mickey Mouse** strip "by Walt Disney" and your name was never mentioned?

G: No, it really hasn't, because I've always felt that Mickey was Walt's character and not mine, and that he's Studio property and certainly the result of the development of lots and lots of people who couldn't possibly all be given credit for him. Not only that, Walt himself proposed to the Syndicate, back around the late '40s, that we be allowed to sign our names to the strips. The Syndicate threw up their hands in horror.

They said no, that one of the big selling points with all their syndicated Disney products was the fact that they were Walt Disney products and that, they said, believe it or not, the bulk of our fans still think that Walt does those himself. They said that the addition of an unknown name would just dilute the sales value of the thing and, of course, that made sense. For that reason, it really hasn't bothered me. I did feel that when specific fans, who knew I had drawn the strips and wanted originals—not only because they were **Mickey** originals but because I had drawn them—it would have been legitimate for me to autograph the things to those fans. I thought it was just a good public relations thing, and to have it denied was, to me, bad public relations for the Studio. But, through the years Frank objected to it. I think a lot of this stemmed from a jealousy thing that grew up when he first came here—the fact that I had managed the department for nearly 17 years. Most of the people on the lot thought of me as the head of the department for maybe five or six years after Frank came. They'd come to me for information instead of him, and I'd send them to him, and he wouldn't have the information. He would have to send them back to me, and then finally he got so that he'd come and ask me what he wanted to know and then go back and pass it on as his information.

S: When did the **Mickey** strip have its peak?

G: As far as I know, the peak in the strip probably was around the early 1940s. I've never seen the actual figures, because I've never been inter-

ested in them, but I remember Roy Disney came to me in the early '40s and told me that the revenue from the Comic Strip Department was keeping the Studio going at that time. The revenue had to be big to make that kind of a difference with the Studio, so I assume about that time was the peak. As you know, television came in about 1947 and by the early 1950s it was beginning to affect newspapers very strongly. It has hurt all the comic strips in the whole industry.

S: Since you worked with both Walt and Roy Disney, how did the two men differ?

G: Roy was always a very warm, friendly, down-to-earth sort of person who never exhibited any harshness in his character. Walt, on the other hand, could be harsh. He was the one-track-minded sort of a fellow who when he got onto a project the only thing that mattered was that project. And it had to be done right. If it wasn't done right, it had to be done over. Whatever he had to do with a person to get it done over, that to him was completely legitimate. I don't think it ever occurred to him that he was being mean to the person on a personal basis. It was just a matter that he had visualized this thing this way, and he knew it wouldn't be right unless it was done that way. And these personalities who did it for him were, in a way, machines. They were technical devices to achieve this thing that had to be done. Roy was more aware of personal feelings. It just didn't occur to Walt to operate that way. And yet in many ways Walt could do great things, make great gestures to people and

Mickey's tail was deleted from the strip during the later part of World War II. Walt had the animators drop it because, according to Gottfredson, "it would save time in animation" when the staff had been severely cut back. But it was reinstated after the war, Gottfredson added, "and we've had it with us ever since. I don't know if anyone ever noticed, but as far as I know, we've never had any fan mail or comments on it."

do great things for them, but he did it when he wanted to do it, when he felt it was the right way to do it, and he felt that if making this gesture to a person would interfere with the project that he was on, then he wouldn't do it. Because the project had to come first. Walt, in my opinion, had a lot of Harry Truman in him; they both had one-track minds. When Walt got on a project, all he saw was the tracks that led to the culmination of it, and he worked accordingly.

S: Did Roy make gestures to people more often than Walt did?

G: Yes, he did. To give you a good insight of what Roy's character was—back in the 1930s while some of us were playing baseball on the hill across from the Hyperion Studio at lunchtime, Roy Disney himself came across the street and called me. He told me that my wife and young son had been in an automobile accident out in West L.A. They weren't hurt, but our car was ruined. Roy said, "I'm going to have Bill Garity drive you out there." Bill was our electrical engineer here at the Studio then, and a pretty important guy. As I've said earlier, the Studio had only one vehicle, the little Ford pickup. Roy said, "I want you to keep the car over the weekend, until you get your affairs worked out." And I said, "But what about Bill?" He said, "Bill can come back on the streetcar. You keep the car—you're going to need it more than Bill Garity or Walt or me or the Studio. You bring it in Monday." He insisted, and that's what I did. This is the kind of character he was, and I've thought about that through the years. How many bosses would have done that? I had only been there a little over a year. Another thing they did that always impressed me—it was a small thing, but I came to work on December 19th, and about five days

after that Roy brought around Christmas cards to everybody, and mine had a five-dollar gold piece in it. Well, that was almost like fifty dollars in those days. And a gold piece! I was so impressed that I never forgot it. It just seemed a great gesture for him.

S: Did you socialize with Walt and Roy?

G: Definitely. My wife Mattie and I used to play bridge with Walt and his wife, Roy and his wife—Bert Gillett and his wife were there, and Ben Sharpsteen and his wife. That culminated in a strange kind of way, which is another indication of Walt's personality. He came to me one time to ask me if we played bridge, and I told him yes we did. He asked us if we would like to come over and I agreed. So we did, and then about a month later Walt asked me again. My wife was about seven months pregnant with our last son

then, and the day that he asked us to come, we were moving and Mattie was taking care of the move. I explained to Walt that with the move, and her condition, she would probably be too tired to come that night. I asked Walt for a rain check, saying as soon as we were settled we'd be glad to come again. He never asked us again. That was the end of it.

S: Floyd, what would you say are the qualifications for a comic strip writer and artist and how do they differ from those for animators?

G: I think to start with, they have to have been comic strip fans. They should have grown up on the comic strips so that they are aware of the deep background of the business, aware of the format, and aware of the way gags and stories are presented. I feel that way about both writers and artists. If they don't have this background, they're going to be inhibited. They should also have a certain knowledge of writing and construction, presentation of gags, and ability to put over points, to write humor so that it will get across, and have to be able to adapt it to the comic strip format, which is a limited format compared to animation. Now the difference between those people working in animation and people in comic strips is that a comic strip artist has to be a layout man and a character artist. People who have tried to move from animation to comic strips usually find they cannot lay out a scene so that it will go over in the couple of minutes that a reader takes to read it, and a good layout man who can present the scene well can't draw the characters well enough. For the same reason, the comic strip artist would find it very hard to move into animation.

S: Thank you, Floyd.

Seated: former comics editor, Chase Craig; Mickey and Donald comics artists, Floyd Gottfredson, Carl Barks, Manuel Gonzales, and Jack Hannah. Standing (extreme left and right): comics publishers, Bruce Hamilton and Russ Cochran. Standing (center): from The Walt Disney Company, Doug Hindley, Wendall Mohler, Wayne Morris, and Tom Golberg. Pasadena, California, 1982.

MICKEY MOUSE

in

BLAGGARD CASTLE

November 12, 1932 – February 10, 1933

114

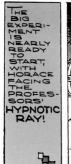

With Mickey wandering helplessly through Blaggard Mansion, Horace Horsecollar faces the most dangerous machine ever invented—the Hypnotic Ray! If it is successful the evil professors, Ecks and Doublex, will be able to hypnotize everybody on Earth—and rule the world! If it fails, Horace's brain will be burned——and he will lose his mind forever! What a horrible, horrible mess!

All right, Professor Ecks! Here it goes!

If it works, we'll be rulers——kings——emperors! The world is ours!

WHIRRRR

CRACKLE SNAP

Z-Z-Z-Z!

WHIRRRR!

That hypnotic ray! I wonder if I—— I wonder if—— I wonder——I—— Ohhhhhhh!

WHIRRR!

G-Gosh! Listen! I know something's happened to Horace! Oh, if only I could find him!

WHIRRR BZZZZZ

Yes, Sheriff! Both Mickey and Horace——you've gotta find 'em!

And——please——we're scared! Don't let them get hurt, will you?

Quick! Get every officer in the state! Notify police cars! Send descriptions by radio! Get out handbills! Bloodhounds! They must be found!

The entire state joins in the search for Mickey and Horace!

NOTICE
MISSING!

No clues yet to missing men! Double your efforts! They must be found!

POLICE BROADCASTING STATION

Calling all cars! Keep a sharp lookout! Pick up any suspicious strangers—that is all!

P.D 333

Have you any news yet, Sheriff?

I'm sorry! We'll let you know when something turns up!

232

That guy's so dumb he couldn't catch measles!

Well, they must be somewhere——and if he doesn't find them soon, I will!

Horace still faces the powerful and terrible hypnotic ray!

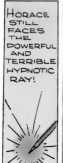

He ought to be hypnotized by now, Prof. Ecks! Give him his instructions!

Horace Horsecollar! You are in our power! You have forgotten all your past life!

We are your masters——and your only friends! Everyone else is your enemy! Destroy them all!

O.K. Prof. Doublex! Let THAT thought sink home, and then—— we'll see!

121

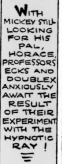

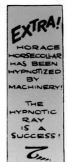

Having turned their hypnotic ray on poor Horace, the professors tell him they are his only friends... that everyone else is his enemy!

He's hypnotized all right. We'll turn him loose in the castle and see if he obeys our instructions!

The wind was whizzing through the trees, how do the holes get in Swiss cheese?

Horace! Horace!

Aha! An enemy to be destroyed!

Take back your heart, thou butcher! I ordered liver!

SOK!

What's the idea o' hittin' me like that?

You are my enemy..... and should be destroyed! My masters told me so!

Your masters!!!

Yes...... Professor Ecks and Professor Doublex!

F' gosh sakes, Horace! What's th' matter? What have they done to you?

Questions! Questions! Always questions!

Life is hard in Russia, but don't drink it while it's too hot! He might bite you! Don't forget...... a word to the wise is worth two in the bush!

Clarabelle! Clarabelle! Look what I found..... in Mickey's waste basket!

Mr. Mickey Mouse
Dear Sir!
We are on the verge of perfecting an amazing invention! But we need your help! Come to the Blaggard Mansion at ten o'clock tonight! We appeal to you in the interest of science! Do not fail us.
Prof. Ecks
Prof. Doublex
Prof. Triplex

Well, for the land's sake! So that's where they've gone!

Shall we tell the Sheriff?

Sheriff Nuthin' he's bungled around long enough! We're gonna investigate this ourselves!

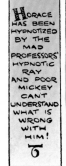

Horace has been hypnotized by the mad professors' hypnotic ray and poor Mickey can't understand what is wrong with him!

Horace! F' gosh sakes, what's th' matter?

That's right! Beefsteak is good for black eyes, but a lawsuit almost never has two pairs of pants!

No! Don't sign anything without reading it! And what are saplings, and how have you been?

B-B-But....

Chairs have four legs, but practically no knees! Why?

Horace! Please stop! Won't ya tell me where you've been?

An alarm clock that goes off is still there, and that is why women leave home, especially when it's smothered in onions!

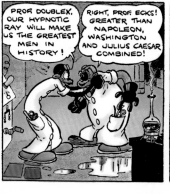

124

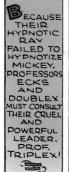

HORACE, BEING HYPNOTIZED, HAS THREATENED TO TAKE MICKEY TO THE EVIL PROFESSORS, ECKS AND DOUBLEX!

HORACE! KEEP AWAY FROM ME!

NOW I'VE GOT YA!

TAG! YOU'RE IT!

NOW YOU CHASE ME!

PROFESSOR TRIPLEX, WHY DID OUR HYPNOTIC RAY WORK ON HORACE, BUT NOT ON MICKEY MOUSE?

THE TWO HAVE DIFFERENT BRAIN STRUCTURES, AND YOUR MACHINE IS NOT YET PERFECT! IT MUST BE CHANGED TO MEET ALL TYPES OF BRAINS!

YOU MUST STUDY THE BRAINS OF MICKEY AND HORACE, AND SEE WHAT THE DIFFERENCE IS!

YES......... BUT HOW WILL WE GET THESE BRAINS?

THAT IS EASY! I WILL GET THEM FOR YOU!

HORACE SAYS TH' HYPNOTIC RAY ROOM HAS A TRAP DOOR THAT DROPS YA DOWN INTO TH' ALLIGATOR PIT!

I DON'T KNOW MUCH ABOUT TRAP DOORS, BUT I DO KNOW THAT IF A DOOR LEADS OUT OF A ROOM, IT ALSO LEADS IN!

TH' TROUBLE THIS TIME IS T' GET TO TH' DOOR IN TH' FIRST PLACE!

AN' THOSE PROFESSORS SURE DIDN'T PUT WELCOME ON TH' DOORMAT!

HORACE SAYS TH' HYPNOTIC RAY ROOM IS RIGHT OVER THIS PIT!

TH' TRAP DOOR IS PROB'LY IN THERE, SOMEWHERE! BUT HOW'LL I EVER GET TO IT? THAT'S TH' TROUBLE!

F'GOSH SAKES! LOOK! THERE'S A LEDGE RUNNING AROUND IT!

WELL...... IF I'VE GOTTA, I'VE GOTTA!

WALT DISNEY

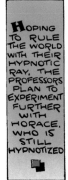

MICKEY HAS STARTED THE HEAT RAY AND BLAGGARD MANSION WILL BE BLOWN UP IN LESS THAN FIVE MINUTES!

C'MON' HURRY! WE'VE GOTTA GET OUT O' HERE!

HOT DIGGETY! WE'RE SAFE! AND WE'VE GOT TWO MINUTES TO SPARE!

YOO-HOO! MICKEY! WAIT FOR US!!!

G-G-GOSH! MINNIE AND CLARABELLE!

MINNIE AND CLARABELLE ARE STILL IN BLAGGARD MANSION! AND IN LESS THAN A MINUTE, IT WILL BE BLOWN INTO A MILLION PIECES! ▽

HEY! HURRY! RUN! DOWN TO TH' FRONT DOOR! QUICK! GET OUT O' THERE!

G-G-GOSH, I HOPE THEY MAKE IT IN TIME!

BOOM!

WELL, FOR TH' LAND SAKES! YOU MIGHT AT LEAST HAVE WAITED TILL WE GOT TH' DOOR OPEN!

OH, BOY! I'M GLAD TO SEE YOU!

WELL, BLOWIN' UP A HOUSE UNDER US IS A FUNNY WAY T' SHOW IT!

BUT WHAT HAPPENED, MICKEY? DID YOU AND HORACE GET INTO ANY TROUBLE?

NOT MUCH! THAT IS, NUTHIN' T' SPEAK OF!

DON'T LET 'IM KID YA! IF IT WASN'T FOR MICKEY, WE'D O' BEEN IN PLENTY O' TROUBLE!

AW, SHUCKS! HUH! C'MON! LET'S GO HOME!

.....AND THAT'S WHY WE BLEW UP TH' CASTLE!

BUT WHAT HAPPENED TO THE PROFESSORS AFTER YOU HYPNOTIZED THEM?

I MADE 'EM FORGET THEY'D EVEN HEARD OF A HYPNOTIC RAY! AN' THEY'RE SWELL FELLOWS, NOW!

WHERE DID THEY GO?

TO A BIG LABORATORY, WHERE THEY'LL STILL BE INVENTING THINGS...... BUT THEY'LL BE FOR PEOPLE INSTEAD OF AGAINST 'EM!

AN' I GUESS THAT'S ABOUT ALL THERE IS TO TELL!

...... AND SO ENDS MICKEY'S ADVENTURE WITH THE THREE PROFESSORS, ECKS, DOUBLEX AND TRIPLEX! LET'S HOPE HE NEVER AGAIN HAS SUCH A SCARY ONE!

MICKEY MOUSE

in

PLUTO AND THE DOGCATCHER

February 11–February 25, 1933

135

MICKEY MOUSE
THE MAIL PILOT

MICKEY, I'VE BEEN AWF'LY WORRIED ABOUT YOU LATELY WHY DON'T YOU SETTLE DOWN AND STUDY SOME KIND OF PROFESSION?

AW, GEE MINNIE! I'VE BEEN HAVIN' A SWELL TIME!

I KNOW, BUT IT SCARES ME! YOU'VE HAD SUCH TERRIBLE ADVENTURES! WHY DON'T YOU BE A DOCTOR, OR A BANKER, OR A LAWYER ···OR···OR··· A MINISTER?

JUST BE ANYTHING, SO LONG AS IT'S QUIET, AND RESPECTABLE AND SAFE! WON'T YOU DO THAT?

SURE, MINNIE, IF I COULD JUST······

??

GEE! I'VE GOT IT! TH' VERY THING!

I'LL BE AN AIRPLANE PILOT!

NO FOOLIN', MINNIE. I'M GONNA START RIGHT AWAY AN' LEARN TO FLY!

BUT... BUT... IS IT SAFE?

AIRPORT

SURE IT IS! I'M GONNA BE AN AIR-MAIL PILOT, ON ACCOUNT OF THAT'S TH' SAFEST KIND THERE IS!

YA SEE, TH' GOVERNMENT IS AWFUL PARTIC'LAR ABOUT ITS MAIL AN' THEY GET TH' VERY SWELLEST PLANES THEY CAN BUY!

WELL···· HERE WE ARE! LET'S GO!

AIRPLANE SCHOOL ENROLL HERE

AIRPLANE SCHOOL

February 27–June 10, 1933

139

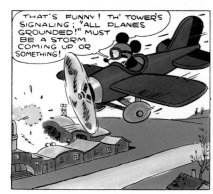

151

Mickey faces his worst enemies, Pete and Shyster, aboard the pirate dirigible, high in the air

But.... I left you two in th' jungle, on that cannibal island!

We didn't stay THERE long! We built a signal fire, and after a week or so, a boat picked us up!

It was a salvage boat, equipped to raise sunken ships! And we had good luck! We found two that were loaded with gold! We were RICH!

They let you share with 'em?

Heh! Heh! Heh! We did better than THAT! Pete and I started a mutiny, made the officers walk the plank, and then I was captain!

Why.... why---- you dirty crooks!

Tell 'im de rest, Shyster! He'll never live t' tell nobody! Haw! Haw! Haw!

Mickey listens in amazement while Pete and Shyster tell him how they escaped from the cannibal island and captured a salvage ship.

Then we sailed up in the North Sea to search for sunken ships, and our diver found three dirigibles, which we raised!

We had an inventor aboard, so he took all the parts and built this airship we're on now!

We have our own crew, we make our own clouds, and we can stay up for MONTHS! And nobody on earth will ever know we're here!

Well, don't forget, Shyster, I know you're here!

Very true... but YOU'LL never be on EARTH! Heh - Heh - Heh!

The arch-criminals, Pete and Shyster, take Mickey for an inspection tour of their huge pirate dirigible

This is our farm. We raise our own vegetables, and fresh milk and meat!

But wait till you see our village! We've got our own stores and markets and even factories!

WELCOME TO PLUNDERVILLE
PATRONIZE HOME INDUSTRY
ROTARY CLUB MEETS TUESDAYS

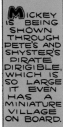
Mickey is being shown through Pete's and Shyster's pirate dirigible, which is so large it even has a miniature village on board.

This is the city of Plunderville. It has every modern convenience. ...including high taxes!

Yeah! Ten thousand feet high! Haw! Haw! Haw!

Well f' gosh sakes!

BOMBS-MACHINE GUNS AND TOBACCO
HABERDASHERY MEN'S CLOTHES AND PARACHUTES
SOFT DRINKS BEER
MEDICO DENTAL BLDG HOSPITAL
CITY HALL
PLUNDERVILLE PUBLIC MARKET LAUNDRY
DRUGS REAL ESTATE - GAS ELECTRICITY - WATER POST OFFICE

HAVING HAD NOTHING TO EAT FOR TWO DAYS, MICKEY IS LED INTO PETE'S AND SHYSTER'S PRIVATE DINING-ROOM ON THE PIRATE DIRIGIBLE.

OH, BOY! I'M HUNGRY!

I HOPES YUH LIKE TH' BUN, MICKEY! IT'S ALL YUH'RE GONNA GIT!

FTOOIE!

WHY, YOU BIG—! IT'S FULL O' COTTON!

HAW! HAW! HAW! WE THOUGHT WE OUGHT T' STUFF YUH FULL O' COTTON, SO WHEN WE DUMP YUH OVERBOARD, YUH WON'T BOUNCE SO HARD!

WHAT ARE YOU GONNA DO WITH TH' MAIL PILOTS YOU'RE HOLDING ON THIS DIRIGIBLE?

NOTHING... ...YET!

BUT DEAD MEN TELL NO TALES! SO WE'RE HEADED FOR A LONELY SPOT, WHERE WE CAN DISPOSE OF THEM WITHOUT LEAVING ANY TRACES!

BUT DON'T WORRY! WE WOULDN'T THINK OF THROWING YOU OVER WITH THE REST!

O' COURSE NOT! HAW! HAW! HAW!

GEE! THANKS! THAT'S GOOD!

YEAH! SWELL! WE'RE GONNA KICK YOU OFF RIGHT NOW!

WITH MICKEY IN THEIR POWER, ABOARD THE PIRATE DIRIGIBLE, PETE AND SHYSTER MAKE HURRIED ARRANGEMENTS TO DISPOSE OF HIM!

WELL, MICKEY, MUCH AS WE HATE TO DO IT... HEH, HEH, HEH... IT'S TIME TO SAY GOOD-BYE!

WE AIN'T GONNA DO NUTHIN'! BUT YOU'RE GONNA WALK THUH PLANK!

WH-WH-WHAT ARE YA GONNA DO?

YUH LIVED THROUGH IT ON SHIPBOARD! BUT WE'RE UP 10,000 FEET... AN' LET'S SEE YUH LIVE THROUGH IT THIS TIME!

AND TO MAKE DOUBLY SURE, WE'LL TIE A BOMB TO YOU THAT WILL EXPLODE WHEN YOU LIGHT!

GANGPLANK

REVENGE AT LAST! PETE AND SHYSTER TIE A BOMB TO MICKEY'S SHOULDERS, AND FORCE HIM OUT ONTO THE DIRIGIBLE'S GANGPLANK!

WE'RE ONLY UP TEN THOUSAND FEET, MICKEY! HEH-HEH-HEH!

GIT GOIN', YUH RAT!

NO MATTER WHAT HAPPENS, I'M NOT GOING TO LET 'EM KNOW I'M SCARED!

WELL... SO LONG, FELLOWS! THANKS FOR YOUR HOSPITALITY!

FORCED TO WALK THE PLANK OFF THE PIRATE DIRIGIBLE, MICKEY GRITS HIS TEETH, WAVES GOOD-BYE AND MAKES A PERFECT DIVE INTO TEN THOUSAND FEET OF SPACE WITH A BOMB TIED TO HIS BACK!

WELL.... I GUESS THIS IS THE END O' **ME**! IF ONLY I COULD HAVE SAID GOOD-BYE TO MINNIE!

THE LAST TIME I SAW HER, I WAS JUST LEAVIN' FOR MY FIRST AIR-MAIL FLIGHT! AN' SHE GAVE ME A KISS!

AN'.... AN'... AN'. GOOD-GOSH! SHE GAVE ME A SILK PARACHUTE, TOO! IT'S IN MY POCKET NOW!

OH, BOY! OH, BOY! OH, **BOY**! DID I GET OUT O' **THAT** MESS? WHOOPEE!

HAVING BEEN MADE TO WALK THE PLANK FROM A DIRIGIBLE, HIGH IN THE AIR, MICKEY OPENS A TINY PARACHUTE MINNIE HAD MADE FOR HIM, AND------

GOSH! I'M SURE GLAD T' GET RID O' THIS BOMB PETE AN' SHYSTER TIED ONTO ME!

THERE SHE GOES!.....AN' THAT'S WHERE I'D BE, TOO, IF THOSE CROOKS HAD KNOWN I HAD THIS PARACHUTE WITH ME!

BOOM!

HOT DIGGETY! THERE COMES AN AIRPLANE! AN' IT'S HEADED RIGHT THIS WAY!

GOIN' MY WAY, BUDDY?

OH, BOY! HE'S CIRCLING AROUND WAITING TO SEE WHERE I LAND!

WELL, FOR---! IT'S MICKEY MOUSE!

YEAH, BUT DON'T WASTE TIME TALKIN'! TAKE ME BACK TO THE AIRPORT.... QUICK!

I CAN JUST SEE PETE AN' SHYSTER, CONGRATULATING EACH OTHER 'CAUSE THEY THINK THEY FINISHED ME! WHAT A SURPRISE **THEY'RE** GONNA GET!

HOME AT LAST! AND THE AIRPORT CERTAINLY LOOKS GOOD TO MICKEY

HI, GLOOMY!

WELL, FER TH'.... EF IT AIN'T MICKEY MOUSE!

DID YA SEE TH' SPIDER?

THAT'S NOT **HALF**! I SAW TH' SPIDER, AN' CAPTAIN DOBERMAN AN'... AN'.

ONLY I CAN'T TALK TO YOU NOW! I'VE GOTTA SEE GENERAL SCHNAUZER QUICK!

MICKEY MOUSE REPORTING, SIR! AN' TH' MAIL'S **GONNA** GO THROUGH!

The entire airport is in an uproar over Mickey's story of Pete and Shyster's pirate dirigible! And every available pilot has been given his instructions!

To your planes, men! We'll sweep the skies of these pirates!

So long, Mickey! Keep yer nose out o' th' propeller!

So long, Gloomy!

AIR MAIL

A wireless message, your highness...from your spy, QT-13, at the airport!

They have probably just received word of Mickey's death! Heh-heh-heh! Let me see it!

Pete! Look what it says! He's still alive!

PLUNDERLAND RADIO SERVICE, LTD
SYLVESTER SHYSTER PRES
PEG-LEG PETE VICE-PRES

MICKEY MOUSE IS LEADING A HUNDRED FIGHTING PLANES TO CAPTURE YOUR DIRIGIBLE BE PREPARED FOR BATTLE.

QT-13

Commander Hairlip calling all planes! Separate and patrol fifty-mile areas allotted to you! Advise all planes by radio if you sight dirigible!

Calling all planes! We are getting close! Go at once to designated posts, and patrol fifty miles apart!

Keep sharp lookout for pirate dirigible! If you sight it, notify all other planes by radio immediately!

Yeah! An' if ya see a funny-lookin' cloud LOOK OUT! I'm tellin' ya!

With a hundred fighting planes after their dirigible, Pete and Shyster are getting worried!

Lissen, Shyster, let's dump them forty mail pilots overboard!

Not yet, Pete! I'll tell you when!

The law says that if there's no dead man, there wasn't any murder! And if these pilots aren't ever FOUND, we're as innocent as babies! See?

So we'll fly over a secluded spot, and then..... heh-heh-heh!

Gosh, I hope one o' th' planes finds that dirigible pretty soon! I've got a hunch there's no time t' LOSE!

THE PIRATE DIRIGIBLE IS STILL AT LARGE! BUT A HUNDRED PLANES, SCATTERED FIFTY MILES APART, ARE COMBING THE AIR FOR IT!

NO NEWS YET, BUT.....

G·G·GOSH! THERE'S A BLACK CLOUD, 'WAY OFF IN TH' DISTANCE!

I DON'T KNOW WHETHER THAT'S TH' DIRIGIBLE OR NOT, BUT YOU BET I'M GONNA FIND OUT!

WHAT DO WE CARE ABOUT A HUNDRED PLANES? OR A THOUSAND? WE'VE GOT ENOUGH GUNS ABOARD TO SHOOT THEM ALL DOWN!

NOW YER TALKIN', SHYSTER! BUT FIRST WE'VE GOTTA THROW DEM PILOTS OVERBOARD!

RIGHT, PETE! AND IN FIVE MINUTES WE'LL BE OVER THE OCEAN! AND THEN........ HEH·HEH·HEH....... GOOD·BYE, PILOTS!

YES, SIR! I'LL BET TH' DIRIGIBLE'S IN THAT CLOUD! BUT I WON'T RADIO TH' REST O' TH' PLANES TILL I'M SURE!

I'LL SNEAK UP ON IT FROM BELOW, 'CAUSE I DON'T WANT T' WARN 'EM!

GOOD GOSH! MAN OVERBOARD!

IT'S CAPTAIN DOBERMAN!

MICKEY! SAVE ME!

O.K. WAIT RIGHT THERE!

INVESTIGATING A BLACK CLOUD TO SEE WHETHER IT CONTAINED THE PIRATE DIRIGIBLE, MICKEY SEES CAPTAIN DOBERMAN PLUNGE OUT OF IT!

A POWER DIVE'S MY ONLY CHANCE TO CATCH HIM! COME ON, PLANE! DON'T FAIL ME NOW!

HOT DIGGETY! I'M GAININ'!

HI, CAPTAIN DOBERMAN! IMAGINE MEETING YOU HERE!

HAVING DISCOVERED THE DIRIGIBLE AND RESCUED CAPTAIN DOBERMAN, MICKEY'S NEXT JOB IS TO NOTIFY THE SQUADRON OF PLANES BY RADIO!

CALLING ALL PLANES! MICKEY MOUSE CALLING ALL PLANES! HEY! WHERE ARE YA?

THAT'S FUNNY! THEY DON'T ANSWER! MEBBE SOMETHING'S WRONG WITH THE RADIO!

WILL YA LOOK AT THE SENDING APPARATUS? IT'S THERE IN THE REAR COCKPIT!

IS THIS IT?

GEE, MICKEY, I'M SORRY I FELL ON YOUR RADIO!

IT WASN'T YOUR FAULT! YOU **HAD** TO LAND **SOMEWHERE!**

WHAT'LL WE DO—— FLY FOR HELP?

IF WE DID, PETE AN' SHYSTER WOULD PUSH TH' REST O' TH' PILOTS OVERBOARD BEFORE WE COULD GET BACK!

POOR, BRAVE FELLOWS! THEY HAVEN'T A CHANCE! NOTHING CAN SAVE THEM NOW! THEY'RE **SUNK!**

SUNK **NUTHIN!** HANG ONTO YER SEAT! WE'RE GONNA GO UP AN' ATTACK THAT DIRIGIBLE BY **OURSELVES!**

NOT KNOWING THEIR PIRATE DIRIGIBLE HAS BEEN LOCATED BY MICKEY, PETE AND SHYSTER PREPARE TO DUMP THE CAPTIVE MAIL PILOTS OVERBOARD!

THE FLOOR OF THEIR CELL IS A TRAP-DOOR! WHEN WE PULL THIS LEVER BACK, IT **OPENS!** HEH-HEH-HEH!

WE'RE ONLY UP 10,000 FEET! IT WON'T HURT 'EM...**MUCH!** HAW! HAW! HAW!

ALL RIGHT, PETE! YOU PULL IT WHEN I COUNT THREE! ONE!...TWO!...

THERE SHE IS—— 'WAY DOWN BELOW!

O, K., MICKEY! LET 'ER GO!

PLANNING TO SEND THE CAPTURED MAIL PILOTS TO THEIR DEATH, PETE STANDS BY THE RELEASE LEVER WHILE SHYSTER COUNTS TO **THREE!**

ONE!

TWO!

THR...

GOOD GOSH! WHAT'S **THAT?**

MACHINE GUNS! WE'RE **ATTACKED!**

SPAT! SPAT! SPAT!

HERE'S WHAT I THINK O' **YOU**——AN' I'M SAYIN' IT WITH **LEAD!**

RAT-A-TAT! RAT-A TAT-TAT! TAT-A TAT-TAT!

THE FLOWERS WILL COME **LATER!**

LOOK OUT, MICKEY! THAT GUN'S GOT OUR RANGE!

WELL, I'LL PUT A STOP TO **THAT!**

BANG!

HOT DIGGETY! LOOK AT 'EM RUN!

RAT-A-TAT A-TAT-TAT!!

THERE'S **ONE** GUN THAT WON'T BOTHER US ANY MORE!

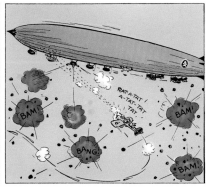

158

MICKEY MOUSE

OUTWITS
THE PHANTOM BLOT

May 20–September 9, 1939

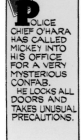

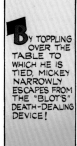

MICKEY HAS CONCOCTED A NEW SCHEME, THE SUCCESS OF WHICH DEPENDS ON LURING THE "BLOT" INTO A CHASE!

McZOOKAS' PHOTO SHOPPE

I'LL HAFTA START WITH A BIT OF BURGLARY, BUT I CAN FIX THAT UP LATER!

I HOPE THE "BLOT" GETS BLAMED FOR THIS!

AH-- HERE WE ARE! HIS FAVORITE BRAND!

NOW TO GO OUT SOME PLACE WHERE HE CAN SEE ME! AND I HOPE HE DOESN'T KEEP ME WAITIN' TOO LONG!

ARMED WITH CAMERAS OF THE MAKE THE "BLOT" IS AFTER, MICKEY HOPES TO ATTRACT HIS ATTENTION AND LURE HIM INTO A CHASE.

MICKEY DOESN'T KNOW THAT THE VILLAIN HAS ALREADY BEEN TRAILING HIM!

FUNNY HE HASN'T SHOWN UP! THE COPS CLAIM HE CAN EVEN SMELL THESE CAMERAS!

ANOTHER HOUR GONE! DARN IT, I DON'T B'LIEVE HE'S COMIN'!

PARDON ME. BUT THIS IS RATHER BORING! JUST WHAT ARE YOUR PLANS?

MICKEY'S PLAN TO LEAD THE "BLOT" INTO CHASING HIM SUCCEEDS ONLY TOO WELL!

IF YOU DON'T MIND TELLING ME, JUST WHAT ARE YOU UP TO?

OMIGOSH--- HE'S HERE!!

HE CAN RUN, TOO, BY GOLLY!

DOES IT BOTHER YOU IF SOMEONE LOOKS OVER YOUR SHOULDER WHILE YOU DRIVE?

ALTHOUGH MICKEY PURPOSELY LED THE "BLOT" INTO A CHASE, HE DID NOT MEAN IT TO BE QUITE SO CLOSE!

WOW!!

OH, DON'T MIND ME! JUST KEEP ON GOING!

AND HOW---!

WALT DISNEY

168

Secure in a secret hideout beneath his real home, Mickey prepares to give the baffling camera mystery everything he's got, determined to find the solution!

THE FIRST THING TO DO ---I GOTTA HAVE A DISGUISE! WHAT'LL IT BE?

AH--- JUST THE TICKET! NOBODY'D KNOW ME IN THIS--- I HOPE!

WHEE! I'M A SUCCESS!

MICKEY MOUSE

Mickey leaves his secret hideout disguised as an old man. He feels his get-up must be a success when Pluto angrily chases him out of the yard!

DON'T BE SKEERED MISTER--- THAT FLEA-BURNER WON'T BITE!

OH-OH--- IT'S HORACE! ANOTHER TEST FOR MY DISGUISE!

MICKEY MOUSE

SORRY, MISTER! HE'S GEN'RALLY WELL-BEHAVED! B'LONGS TO MICKEY MOUSE BUT HE'S OUTA TOWN AN'---!

NEVER MIND THE EXCUSES! I'D JUST LIKE TO MEET THIS MOUSE PERSON ONCE! IT'S AN OUTRAGE, THAT'S WHAT IT IS!

OH, BOY--- HORACE ISN'T LOOKIN'!

PLUTO! GO HOME!!

GOOD GRAVY--- I BETTER SEE A DOCTOR! I COULD 'A SWORN I HEARD MICKEY!

OH, BOY! HERE'S A CHANCE TO TRY MY DISGUISE ON GOOFY!

GOOD MORNIN', GOOFY!

MORNIN', MR. SCHULTZ!

--ER, I MEAN-- MR. BURGHEIMER---!

--ER, MR.--- HUH? WHY, GAWRSH-DING IT, I DON'T KNOW THET FELLER ATALL!

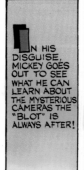

In his disguise, Mickey goes out to see what he can learn about the mysterious cameras the "BLOT" is always after!

THIS IS WHERE THE DEALERS GET 'EM FROM! I'LL PRETEND I'VE GOT A STORE, TOO!

MAGOOKUS & CO. JOBBERS IN CAMERAS AND SUPPLIES WHOLESALE ONLY

WHAT FOR KIND OF CAMERAS IS THESE YOU SELL ME? CHEAP LIKE JUNK, YET MY STORE GETS ROBBED FROM THEM!

TAKE IT EASY, MISTER! YOUR STORE'S NOT THE ONLY ONE!

SO WHAT? DOES IT HELP ME BECAUSE BLACK CROOKS ROB OTHERS? WHY, I INQUIRE --- WHY?

LOOK, BROTHER-- WE ONLY SELL 'EM! THEY'RE AN IMPORTED MAKE! IF YOU WANT TO TAKE IT UP WITH THE FACTORY---!

I SHALL DO SO! I SHALL CABLEGRAM IMMEDIATE! I HAVE STOOD SUFFICIENT!

WALT DISNEY

172

UNABLE TO GET RID OF THE NOOSE THE "BLOT" PUT AROUND HIS NECK, MICKEY STARTS FOR HOME, ONLY TO BE PINCHED AS AN ATTEMPTED SUICIDE! POLICE CHIEF O'HARA COMES TO HIS RESCUE.

THERE Y' ARE, MICKEY! YOU'RE OUT O' THAT JAM, ANYWAY!

THANKS, MR. O'HARA! AND I'M STILL IN THIS CASE WITH BOTH FEET!

I'M DURN GLAD YE ARE-- THINGS ARE LOOKIN' MIGHTY BLACK! THE "BLOT'S" RUNNIN' WILD --EVEN GRABBIN' CAMERAS FROM PEOPLE ON THE STREETS IN BROAD DAYLIGHT!

THE WHOLE POLICE DEPARTMENT'S ON THE PAN-- EVERYBODY'S JUMPIN' ON US AT ONCE!

GETTIN' HOT, IS IT? DOGGONE IT, THAT "BLOT" CAN'T GET AWAY WITH THIS FOREVER!

WELL, BE CAREFUL, LAD-- HE'S PLENTY SLICK AND SHARP!

SO'S AN ICICLE --TILL Y' TURN ON THE HEAT!

MICKEY LEAVES THE POLICE CHIEF'S OFFICE, FULL OF RENEWED PEP AND DETERMINED THAT THE "BLOT" HAS BEEN GETTING AWAY WITH THINGS LONG ENOUGH!

FIRST THING, I'LL SEE IF THERE'S AN ANSWER TO MY CABLE TO THE CAMERA FACTORY!

CAL...
INTER-...
MR EMANUEL SPINK MOUSEVILLE, U.S.A.

NOTHING IN OUR CAMERAS THAT WOULD INTEREST CRIMINAL NEW SHIPMENT RECENTLY RECEIVED BY MAMMOTH DEPT. STORE YOUR TOWN. SUGGEST YOU CONTACT THEM.

TRANS-OCEANIC CAMERA CO

--- THAT'S AN IDEA!

I'LL HAFTA GO BACK TO MY HIDEOUT FIRST AND GET A NEW DISGUISE! THE OLD 'BLOT'S' WISE TO THIS ONE NOW!

WELL, I MAY NOT LOOK PRETTY, BUT I SURE LOOK LOUD!

ALL RIGGED OUT IN THE VERY LATEST IN DISGUISES, MICKEY PURSUES HIS INVESTIGATIONS DOWN AT THE MAMMOTH DEPARTMENT STORE!

YOU'RE THE MANAGER, I BELIEVE!

THAT'S RIGHT! OH-- A DETECTIVE! WHAT CAN I DO FOR YOU?

I UNDERSTAND YOU'VE GOT A NEW SUPPLY OF LITTLE KORKER CAMERAS IN STOCK!

YES-- THEY WERE DELIVERED ABOUT A WEEK AGO!

ER-- HAS THIS STOCK BEEN MOLESTED IN ANY WAY, OR---?

YOU MEAN, BY THAT CRACKPOT IN THE BLACK OUTFIT? NO --AND WE CAN'T FIGURE WHY!

WE'VE HAD 'EM GUARDED DAY AN' NIGHT BECAUSE OUR FIRST SHIPMENT WAS LOOTED ENTIRELY! BUT THESE --- NEVER TOUCHED!

BROTHER, YOU'VE UN-COVERED SOMETHIN'! AT LAST A FAINT LIGHT BEGINS TO FLICKER THROUGH THE CRACKS IN MY DOME!

CHECKING WITH THE MANAGER OF A BIG STORE, MICKEY LEARNS THAT A NEW SHIPMENT OF CAMERAS HAS BEEN ENTIRELY UNMOLESTED BY THE "BLOT!"

THE SAME IDENTICAL MAKE, MIND YOU, BUT HE HASN'T EVEN GIVEN 'EM A TUMBLE!

HM-M-M-- --THIS IS VERY INTERESTIN'!

AND YET I DOUBT IF THERE'S TWO DOZEN OF THE OLD ONE'S STILL IN EXISTENCE! IT BEATS ME!

WELL, THANK YA, SIR--- YOU'VE BEEN A BIG HELP!

MICKEY HUSTLES BACK TO HIS ROOM.

TWO SHIPMENTS OF CAMERAS, BOTH ALIKE-- BUT THE "BLOT" ONLY WANTS THE OLD ONES! HE GETS 'EM-- BUSTS 'EM OPEN! IT-- MUST BE ---!!

WHAT AM I SITTIN' HERE FOR? I'VE GOT THINGS TO DO!

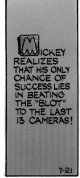

After finally getting the camera that contains the mysterious hidden paper, Mickey is again outwitted by the "BLOT!" The villain forces Mickey's car off the road, crashing it into a tree!

W-WHAT HAPPENED? I FEEL --SICK!

YOU FEEL MARVELOUS --- COMPARED TO HOW YOU WILL FEEL!

FIRST--I'LL TAKE CARE OF THIS DOCUMENT YOU SO KINDLY FOUND FOR ME!

THEN I'LL TAKE CARE OF YOU --- FOR THE LAST TIME!

Y-YOU CAN'T --- GET AWAY --- WITH THIS ---!

YOU HAVE ANNOYED ME TOO LONG, MY FRIEND! FROM THIS DAY ON, MICKEY MOUSE IS BUT A MEMORY!

I STILL SAY Y' WON'T GET AWAY WITH THIS! THE POLICE ARE WITH ME ---!

THE POLICE? HA--HA--HA! YOU MEAN THE CORONER!

SORRY TO HAVE TO DO THIS, BUT "DEAD MEN TELL NO TALES!"

YEH? WELL, I'M STILL PLENTY ALIVE!

OH, THAT'S JUST A TEMPORARY CONDITION --- IT WON'T LAST LONG!

ANYTHING NEW ON THE "BLOT" CASE?

ALL UNDER CONTROL, CHIEF! TH' FIRST MOVE THAT BIRD MAKES, HE'S A GONE GOOSE!

ANOTHER ONE OF YOUR CRACK-BRAINED TORTURE STUNTS, EH! HAVEN'T Y' FOUND OUT THEY NEVER WORK?

THERE WILL BE NO SLIP THIS TIME! I HAVE MADE ARRANGEMENTS THAT GUARANTEE SUCCESS!

SORRY I CAN'T STAY, MYSELF, BUT SINCE YOU FOUND THAT LITTLE PIECE OF PAPER FOR ME, I MUST BE ON MY WAY WITH IT!

THAT PIECE O' PAPER SEEMS TO BE GOSH-AWFUL IMPORTANT!

AH, IT'S WORTH A FORTUNE, MY FRIEND --- A VERY LARGE FORTUNE! NOW, WE CAN TEST THIS OUT IF YOU'LL KINDLY JERK YOUR FOOT A LITTLE!

OH, YOU WON'T DO THAT? WELL I DARESAY YOU WILL AT THE PROPER TIME!

Again captured by the "BLOT," Mickey is forced into another of the villain's infernal devices!

I'M QUITE PROUD OF THIS LITTLE ARRANGEMENT! A HOT FOOT --- A SUDDEN JERK, AND -- BANG!

S'POSIN' IT DOES GET ME, Y' RAT --- TH' COPS 'LL GET YOU!

THE COPS! HA-HA-HA! BY THE TIME THEY FIND YOUR BODY I'LL BE HALFWAY ACROSS THE OCEAN --- WITH THIS!

FAREWELL, MY FRIEND! I REGRET THIS ENDING OF OUR ACQUAINTANCE --- BUT THAT'S LIFE --- AND DEATH!

OW --- THAT'S GETTIN' WARM! BUT IF I MOVE MY FOOT --- GOSH!

ESCAPING MIRACULOUSLY FROM ONE TRAP AFTER ANOTHER, MICKEY IS GROGGY BUT STILL DETERMINED TO KEEP AFTER THE "BLOT!"

HOPE THIS JUNK WILL STILL RUN! HOT DOG-- SHE DOES!

IT'S NOT MY FAULT, SIR! I HAVEN'T GOT A SPEEDBOAT LEFT--- THEY'RE ALL OUT!

STUPID DUNDERHEAD! I'VE WASTED ENOUGH TIME--- GET ME A BOAT!

LUCKILY, I KNOW WHERE TO GO, SINCE HE SO KINDLY BRAGGED ABOUT BEING BOUND FOR THE OCEAN!

GOSH -- THERE HE GOES! I'M JUST AN EYELASH TOO LATE!

CAESAR'S GHOST! I THOUGHT I FINISHED THAT PEST!

WELL, NO MATTER! BEFORE HE CAN TIP OFF "THE POLICE I'LL BE IN MID-OCEAN!

ROWWPH!

FAREWELL, MY FRIEND! TOO BAD YOU MISSED THE BOAT!

WHO--MISSED --- WHAT --- BOAT?

MAKING HIS GETAWAY IN A STOLEN SPEEDBOAT, THE "BLOT" IS AMAZED TO DISCOVER MICKEY CLINGING TO AN AQUAPLANE ATTACHED TO THE STERN!

YOU MEDDLING LITTLE --- I'LL SETTLE YOU!

BANG! BANG! BANG! BANG! BANG! BANG!

EMPTY! THE BLASTED FOOL BEARS A CHARMED LIFE!

CLICK!

CURSE THE LUCK! MUST I ALWAYS BE HAUNTED BY THAT PESTIFEROUS WART?

TUT-TUT, OLD BOY--- YOU'RE LOSIN' YOUR TEMPER!

TAKE YOUR CHOICE, YOU FOOL--- LET GO NOW OR BE DASHED TO PIECES!

DRY DOCK BOAT REPAIRS

YOU ASKED FOR IT!

...EPAIRS

GOOD GOSH --- NO RUDDER!!

Row 1:

THROWN LOOSE FROM THE "BLOT'S" SPEEDBOAT, MICKEY LANDS IN ANOTHER BOAT WHICH STARTS OFF CARRYING HIM THROUGH THE WATER AT A RIOTOUS PACE!

GOOD NIGHT---THIS THING'S GOT NO RUDDER! I CAN'T STEER IT!

8-24

THANKS FOR THE COMEDY, MY FRIEND! I TAKE MY LEAVE WITH A PLEASANT MEMORY!

MY GOSH---NOW HE'S GOT A PLANE! AND WHAT CAN I DO -- WITH THIS?

WALT DISNEY

Row 2:

WHAT SOUR LUCK! HELPLESS IN A BOAT WITH NO RUDDER --- WHILE THE "BLOT" GETS AWAY IN A PLANE!

8-25

I'D ADVISE YOU TO SWIM IT --- YOU'D AT LEAST GET SOMEWHERE!

HEY -- IF WE TURN THIS WAY FAR ENOUGH THERE'S JUST A CHANCE ---!!

Distributed by King Features Syndicate, Inc.

Row 3:

UNKNOWN TO THE "BLOT," WHO IS MAKING HIS ESCAPE IN A PLANE, MICKEY GRABS PART OF THE PLANE AND HOISTS HIMSELF ABOARD!

BOY, AM I LUCKY! ANOTHER SECOND AND HE'D HAVE MADE A CLEAN GETAWAY!

8-26

Y' DON'T KNOW IT, MR. "BLOT," BUT I GOT A PASSENGER WHO WANTS TO GO THE OTHER WAY!

AND, REMEMBER, THE CUSTOMER'S ALWAYS RIGHT --- SO LET'S --- UNH --- TURN AROUND!

THOUSAND NAMES OF A DEVIL! THE SHIP'S OUT OF CONTROL!

WALT DISNEY

Row 4:

APPARENTLY MAKING A SAFE GETAWAY IN A SEAPLANE, THE "BLOT" IS SUDDENLY STARTLED WHEN THE PLANE STARTS TO TURN OUT OF HIS CONTROL!

CURSE THE SHIP --- THE PLAGUY RUDDER MUST BE JAMMED!

8-28

HE DOES NOT KNOW THAT A LITTLE STOWAWAY IS STEERING THE PLANE FROM BEHIND.

RIGHT ON AROUND OL' BOY --- POINT YOUR NOSE FOR HOME!

MEANWHILE, AT POLICE HEADQUARTERS, DETECTIVE CASEY IS READY TO PRESENT HIS COMPLETE CASE TO CHIEF O'HARA!

I'VE GOT THE WHOLE WORKS, CHIEF! FULL DESCRIPTION --- WHERE HE HANGS OUT --- FINGERPRINTS --- EV'RYTHING! I TOLD YA I'D DO IT, DIDN'T I?

SURE, YE TOLD ME --- QUITE FREQUENT! NOW, LET'S HEAR WHAT YE GOT THERE!

WALT DISNEY

183

Seeing the "Blot" bail out of the falling plane, Mickey takes a quick chance and jumps after him!

OH, BOY! JUST LIKE A FIRE-NET!

OUCH! THIS GROUND'S HARD!

YIPPEE --- THAT WASN'T GROUND I HIT! I'VE KNOCKED THE OLD VILLAIN COLD!

While Mickey brings down the "Blot" in a bloodless air battle, Chief O'Hara is still sizzling over Casey's blunder!

GOSH, CHIEF— I DUNNO HOW THEM CLUES GOT CROSSED LIKE THAT---!

CLUES? YE NEVER HAD ANY! YE WERE SO DANGED BUSY SHADOWIN' THE WRONG MAN, YE WOULDN'T KNOW THE "BLOT" IF YE MET 'IM!

B-R-R-R R-RRING!

HELLO? SILAS PERKINS OF STICKLEVILLE -- YES! A CAMERA STOLEN FROM YOUR NIECE? SAY NO MORE, MR. PERKINS, I'LL BE RIGHT OUT!

FOLLOW ME, CASEY! I'M TAKIN' PERSONAL CHARGE OF THIS AND FROM NOW ON THERE'S GOIN' TO BE ACTION!

YES, SIR ---SURE, CHIEF!

BOY! IT'S A PLEASURE FOR ME TO DO THE TYING UP ON THIS GUY! YES, SIR--- A PLEASANT CHANGE!

ARR-R-RH! YOU LITTLE---!

QUIT GROWLIN' AND KEEP MOVIN'!

Not yet knowing of the "Blot's" capture, O'Hara and Casey are speeding out to Stickleville in response to a call!

SHADES O' ME UNCLE'S GHOST! DO YOU SEE WHAT I SEE?

IF I'M AWAKE, I DO!

SKREE-E-E-E!

WELL, I'LL BE---!!

IT'S THE "BLOT!" MICKEY'S GOT HIM!

CAPTURED! The "Blot" is finally brought into custody and at police headquarters he "tells all!"

THIS PAPER THAT WAS THE OBJECT OF THE CRIME WAVE--- YE SAY IT'S A CHEMICAL FORMULA?

THAT'S RIGHT! FOR A MATERIAL SIMILAR TO RADIUM, BUT MUCH CHEAPER!

THIS INVENTION WAS BOUGHT BY A FIRM IN THIS COUNTRY WHO WERE GOING TO FURNISH IT TO HOSPITALS AT COST! BUT A CERTAIN SYNDICATE ABROAD MEANT TO HAVE IT AT ANY PRICE---!

I DON'T GET IT! WHY WOULD THIS SYNDICATE PAY ANY PRICE JUST FOR A CHEAP "CURE," YE MIGHT CALL IT?

AH! BUT ONE KNOWING THE SECRET OF THIS CHEMICAL COULD ALSO ADAPT IT TO WAR MATERIAL MORE POWERFUL THAN ANY KNOWN!

BUT NOW--- I SUPPOSE IT WILL BE USED ONLY FOR PEACE! WHAT A PITY! TSK! TSK!

THE "BLOT'S" CONFESSION TELLS OF BEING THE AGENT FOR A FOREIGN SYNDICATE WHICH WAS AFTER A SECRET FORMULA BEING TAKEN TO AMERICA! ON SHIPBOARD HE HIGH-JACKED THE MESSENGER OF THE VALUABLE PAPER!

BUT, UNFORTUNATELY, DETECTIVES WERE CLOSE UPON ME AND I WAS FORCED TO FLEE! I REACHED THE HOLD OF THE SHIP---!

AND **THAT'S** WHERE Y' HID THE PAPER INSIDE A CAMERA, THINKIN' TO GET IT AGAIN WHEN THE BOAT LANDED?

EXACTLY! BUT I HAD TO HIDE **MYSELF**, AND SO GOT INTO ANOTHER PACKING CASE -- WHICH, AS EVIL LUCK WOULD HAVE IT ---

--- WAS UNLOADED AT THE PIER AND STORED IN A WAREHOUSE! BEFORE I COULD GET OUT, THE CAMERA SHIPMENT---!

I **GOT** IT! BY THAT TIME TH' CAM'RAS HAD ALL GONE TO THE DEALERS! LIKE I ALWAYS SAID---AN **EASY** CASE!

WELL, I GUESS THAT'S ALL! YE PLAYED A DESPERATE GAME WITH THE LAW--- AND YE LOST!

YES--I LOST---!

I LOST BECAUSE OF THE MOST STUBBORN, IDIOTIC, PERSISTENT LITTLE FOOL THAT EVER LIVED! **THAT PEST!**

YOU -- Y' MEAN---?

YES, **YOU!** I SHOULD HAVE FINISHED YOU THE FIRST CHANCE I HAD!

W-WELL, WHY **DIDN'T** Y'--- INSTEAD OF LEAVIN' ME IN THOSE-- THOSE TRAPS?

BECAUSE OF MY CURSED SOFT HEART! I NEVER COULD BEAR TO **SEE** ANYTHING DIE! I'M JUST TOO TENDER FOR SUCH THINGS---!

ENOUGH! TAKE HIM AWAY BEFORE **MY** HEART BREAKS!

MICKEY, THAT'S THE FINEST SERVICE YE EVER DONE THE DEPARTMENT! I'M WRITIN' A LITTLE CHECK ON ME OWN ACCOUNT---!

AW, SHUCKS, MR. O'HARA-- I DON'T WANT ANY-THING!

I **KNOW** YE DON'T, BUT JUST THE SAME--- **OOPS!** DURN THIS PEN!

THAT'S NO GOOD, MICKEY--- LET ME WRITE YE ANOTHER!

NO, **SIR!** THIS IS A PERFECT SOUVENIR TO END THE "BLOT" CASE AND I'M **KEEPIN'** IT!

OKAY, YE CRAZY IDJUT! I HOPE IT'S THE LAST TIME I NEED ANY HELP FROM **YOU!**

THANKS! I HOPE YOU'RE A LIAR, MR. O'HARA!

THE END.

INDEXING THE MOUSE
A Bibliography of Floyd Gottfredson's Adventure Strips

Starting and ending dates, plot synopses, and individual aritst and writer credits compiled by Byron Erickson.

The **Mickey Mouse** daily strip began on January 13, 1930, and regularly featured continuities until late 1955 when the format was changed to gag-a-day at the request of King Features Syndicate. The Sunday page was added beginning on January 10, 1932, and, while there were adventures published in the Sunday pages, continuity was not a week-in, week-out occurrence. It's unclear whether Floyd Gottfredson plotted or helped to plot the Sunday continuities after the first two stories. While it's obvious they have less of the Gottfredson "touch," he always discussed stories with his writers and—as head of the Comic Strip Department—edited all copy submitted to him. Since the focus of this book is on the work of Gottfredson, only those Sunday continuities on which he worked are listed.

Both European and American sources have published "definitive" indexes of Gottfredson's adventures. This publication attempts to resolve much of the controversies surrounding starting and ending dates of the stories, and to include short continuities omitted from other lists. The most difficult task, however, has been selecting from the many titles that have been assigned to the stories over the years. Gottfredson had his own that were never used in print, others appear in Big Little Books or comic books, and still others seem to have evolved from the inspiration of fans. Hopefully, this listing will become definitive.

In regard to the assigning of artist and writer credits to the individual stories, the publishers are indebted to Alberto Becattini and Luca Boschi for their research into the Disney creators.

THE DAILY STRIPS

"Lost on a Desert Island"
1/13–3/31/30—More a loosely connected series of gags than a real story, the plot centers on Mickey's

adventures as a castaway on a desert island inhabited by cannibals, although at the end of these encounters Mickey **walks** home to the farm. Many of the gags—and the opening sequence in which Mickey builds a makeshift plane in his barnyard—were lifted from "Plane Crazy" (released in 1928) and "The Castaway" (released in 1931, although in production at the time the strips were prepared). *Written by Walt Disney, penciled by Ub Iwerks (1/13–2/8) and Win Smith, inked by Win Smith.*

"Mickey Mouse in Death Valley"
4/1–9/20/30—Minnie is named sole heir to her Uncle Mortimer's estate, including a gold mine in Death Valley. Sylvester Shyster, the estate's crooked executor, and Peg-Leg Pete, his none-too-bright henchman, plot to steal the map to the mine. Mickey and Minnie are aided by a mys-

terious character named "The Fox." The scenes set in a haunted house were inspired by "The Haunted House" (1929).
Written by Walt Disney (4/1–5/17) and Floyd Gottfredson; penciled by Win Smith (4/1–5/3), Floyd Gottfredson (5/5–6/7, 6/23–9/20), and Hardie Gramatky [?] (6/9–6/21); inked by Win Smith (4/1–5/3), Floyd Gottfredson (5/5–5/17), Floyd Gottfredson and Hardie Gramatky (5/19–6/7, 6/23–9/20), and Hardie Gramatky (6/9–6/21).

"Mr. Slicker and the Egg Robbers"
9/22–12/26/30—Minnie's father is in danger of losing his egg ranch due to a series of egg thefts and Mickey is accused of the crime. A smooth character named Slicker offers financial aid in exchange for Minnie's hand.
Written and penciled by Floyd Gottfredson, inked by Floyd Gottfredson and Hardie Gramatky (9/22–11/15) and Earl Duvall.

Gag-a-day strips—12/27/30–1/17/31
Written by Floyd Gottfredson (12/27/30, 1/5–1/10/31, 1/16, 1/17) and Earl Duvall (12/29/30–1/3/31, 1/12–1/15), inked by Earl Duvall.

"Mickey Mouse Vs. Kat Nipp"
1/19–2/25/31—This sequence, more gags loosely connected to form a story, features a series of encounters between Mickey and Kat Nipp, a tough neighborhood cat. Their rivalry takes the form of a series of escalation gags in which victory is defined by the number of knots that have been added to the loser's tail.
Written by Floyd Gottfredson, penciled by Floyd Gottfredson (1/19–2/7, 2/14–2/21) and Earl Duvall (2/9–2/13, 2/23–2/25), inked by Earl Duvall.

"Mickey Mouse, Boxing Champion"
2/26–4/29/31—Mickey takes on the job of training Minnie's cousin, Rough House Rat, the heavy-light-weight champ, for a title defense against Creamo Catnera, a local bruiser. When Rough House skips town, Mickey is forced to fight in his place.
Written by Floyd Gottfredson, penciled by Earl Duvall (2/26–2/28) and Floyd Gottfredson, inked by Earl Duvall (2/26–2/28) and Al Taliaferro.

"High Society"

4/30–5/29/31—These strips are a series of gags based on Mickey's attempts to teach manners to an ex-convict named Butch. During the last half of May, the strip offered a free "photo" of Mickey almost every day.
Written and penciled by Floyd Gottfredson, inked by Al Taliaferro.

"Circus Roustabout"

5/30–7/7/31—Mickey joins the circus and gets entangled in the Skeleton Man's plot to destroy the star act, Mlle. Maltese, a bareback equestrienne.
Written and penciled by Floyd Gottfredson, inked by Al Taliaferro.

"Pluto the Pup"

7/8–7/18/31—Pluto debuts in the strip in this short series of related gags.
Written and penciled by Floyd Gottfredson, inked by Al Taliaferro.

"Mickey Mouse and the Gypsies"

7/19–11/7/31—Mickey and Minnie join Horace and Clarabelle on a camping trip to the mountains, but Minnie is kidnaped by a band of Gypsies and held for $5,000 ransom.
Written and penciled by Floyd Gottfredson, inked by Al Taliaferro.

"Fireman Mickey"

11/9–11/30/31—Mickey helps out Pop Weezil, the town's fireman, constable, Justice of the Peace, Postmaster, station agent, etc.
Written and penciled by Floyd Gottfredson, inked by Al Taliaferro.

"Clarabelle's Boarding House"

12/1/31–1/9/32—Clarabelle opens a boarding house and Mickey helps her run it in this loosely connected series of gags.
Written and penciled by Floyd Gottfredson, inked by Al Taliaferro.

"The Great Orphanage Robbery"

1/11–5/14/32—Mickey and the gang put on a benefit performance of **Uncle Tom's Cabin** to  aid the local orphanage. When the proceeds are stolen by Peg-Leg Pete and Sylvester Shyster, Mickey and Horace are accused of the crime. Portions of this story were inspired by "The Klondike Kid" (1932) and "Mickey's Mellerdrammer" (1933).
Written and penciled by Floyd Gottfredson, inked by Al Taliaferro.

"Mickey Mouse Sails for Treasure Island"

5/16–11/11/32—The Widow Churchmouse enlists Mickey's aid in finding a buried treasure—the same treasure hunt her husband undertook years before and from which he never returned. The story contains elements adapted from "Trader Mickey" (1932) and "Shanghaied" (1934).
Written and penciled by Floyd Gottfredson, inked by Al Taliaferro and Ted Thwaites.

"Blaggard Castle"

11/12/32–2/10/33—Mickey and Horace are lured to a deserted mansion by Professors Ecks and Doublex. The mad scientists want them to use as guinea pigs to test a hypnotic ray invented by Professor Triplex with which they hope to rule the

world. The plot was inspired by the 1933 cartoon, "The Mad Doctor."
Plotted and penciled by Floyd Gottfredson, written by Webb Smith, inked by Ted Thwaites.

"Pluto and the Dogcatcher"

2/11–2/25/33—Pluto is pursued by an almost soft-hearted dogcatcher played by Peg-Leg Pete in an uncharacteristic role.
Plotted and penciled by Floyd Gottfredson, written by Ted Osborne, inked by Ted Thwaites.

"The Mail Pilot"

2/27–6/10/33—Mickey decides to enroll in flying school in hopes of becoming a mail pilot. He learns that many planes have disappeared without a trace, and eventually his own plane is swallowed by a huge dirigible owned by Peg-Leg Pete and Sylvester Shyster. Gloomy, the mechanic, and Captain Doberman, later head of the Secret

Service, debut in this story, parts of which were based on "The Mail Pilot" (1933).
Plotted and penciled by Floyd Gottfredson, written by Ted Osborne, inked by Ted Thwaites.

"Mickey Mouse and His Horse Tanglefoot"

6/12–10/7/33—Mickey is tricked into buying a broken-down racehorse named Tanglefoot. The upkeep is so high that he has to win the big steeplechase race or be sent to jail for debt. Basic plot inspiration was provided by the cartoon, "The Steeplechase" (1933).
Plotted and penciled by Floyd Gottfredson, written by Ted Osborne, inked by Ted Thwaites.

"The Crazy Crime Wave"

10/9/33–1/9/34—Dippy Dawg (later Goofy) inherits a detective agency from his uncle and invites Mickey to go into business with him. They are

soon puzzled by a crazy crime wave in which the only things stolen are hair and red flannel underwear.
Plotted and penciled by Floyd Gottfredson, written by Merrill de Maris, inked by Ted Thwaites.

"The Captive Castaways"

1/10–4/17/34—Captain Doberman returns to  ask Mickey to fly food and medicine to the snow-bound town of Rock Ledge. With Minnie along he completes the mission, but on their return they are lost in a storm and blown out to sea where they land on the deck of a smuggling ship run by Peg-Leg Pete.
Plotted and penciled by Floyd Gottfredson, written by Merrill de Maris, inked by Ted Thwaites.

"Pluto's Rival"

4/18–4/28/34—Mickey temporarily adopts a cute puppy who makes Pluto jealous.
Plotted and penciled by Floyd Gottfredson, written by Ted Osborne, inked by Ted Thwaites.

"The Bat Bandit of Inferno Gulch"

4/30–7/28/34—Mickey and Minnie head west for a vacation on Uncle Mortimer's dude ranch only to find the countryside terrorized by a black-clad villain known as the Bat Bandit.
Plotted and penciled by Floyd Gottfredson, written by Ted Osborne, inked by Ted Thwaites.

"Bobo the Elephant"

7/30–10/13/34—Mickey mistakenly buys a baby elephant named Bobo at an auction and it causes him nothing but trouble. However, when Eli Squinch claims the elephant is his, Mickey is reluctant to give it up as Squinch wants Bobo to power his sawmill. Based on "Mickey's Elephant" (1936).
Plotted and penciled by Floyd Gottfredson, written by Ted Osborne, inked by Ted Thwaites.

"The Sacred Jewel"

10/15–12/29/34—Mickey, Minnie, and Dippy are recruited by Captain Churchmouse to help him deliver the Sacred Star of Zwoosh to Caliph Houv-Ya-Ben of Umbrella-stan. The jewel is stolen and Minnie is kidnaped by Pete and Shyster.
Plotted and penciled by Floyd Gottfredson, written by Ted Osborne, inked by Ted Thwaites.

"Pluto the Racer"

12/31/34–3/2/35—When Horace ridicules Pluto, Mickey enters his pet in the Pooch Park dog races and runs afoul of a gambling syndicate.
Plotted and penciled by Floyd Gottfredson, written by Ted Osborne, inked by Ted Thwaites.

"Editor-in-Grief"

3/4–6/1/35—Mickey buys The War-Drum, a run-down newspaper, and begins a crusade against crooked politicians and racketeers led by

Peg-Leg Pete. Donald Duck makes his first appearance in the daily strip as a newsboy.
Plotted and penciled by Floyd Gottfredson, written by Ted Osborne, inked by Ted Thwaites.

"Race for Riches"

6/3–9/28/35—Eli Squinch learns that a map to a cache of gold is hidden in Clarabelle's attic. When he can't sweet-talk her into marrying him, he threatens to foreclose on her mortgage, forcing Mickey and Horace to race after the gold. Squinch is aided by Peg-Leg Pete in trying to stop them and steal the map.
Plotted and penciled by Floyd Gottfredson, written by Ted Osborne, inked by Ted Thwaites.

"The Pirate Submarine"

9/30/35–1/4/36—Mickey hears a mysterious S.O.S. on his shortwave radio and queries Captain Doberman about it. Doberman informs him that many ships are turning up without crew or cargo and convinces Mickey to rejoin the air service to investigate the matter. Aided by Gloomy, his mechanic from "The Mail Pilot," Mickey flies a new "submarplane" in search of the culprit, the evil Dr. Vulter.
Plotted and penciled by Floyd Gottfredson, written by Ted Osborne, inked by Ted Thwaites.

"Oscar the Ostrich"

1/6–3/20/36—Mickey finds a runaway ostrich that wreaks havoc on the town. Faced with either an enormous bill for damages or jail, Mickey

enters Oscar in a screwball animal race. Goofy appears as Goofy for the first time in the dailies in this story.
Plotted and penciled by Floyd Gottfredson, written by Ted Osborne, inked by Ted Thwaites.

"Mickey Mouse Joins the Foreign Legion"

3/21–8/8/36—Mickey is inducted into the Secret Service and travels to North Africa on the trail of Trigger Hawkes and stolen blueprints. He enlists

in the Foreign Legion to keep an eye on Hawkes and runs afoul of Peg-Leg Pete, alias Major Beau Chest.
Plotted and penciled by Floyd Gottfredson, written by Ted Osborne, inked by Ted Thwaites.

"The Seven Ghosts"

8/10–11/28/36—Mickey, Goofy, and Donald form a detective agency and are hired by Col. Bassett to rid his seaside manor of ghosts. The plot is loosely based on the 1937 cartoon short, "Lonesome Ghosts."
Plotted and penciled by Floyd Gottfredson, written by Ted Osborne, inked by Ted Thwaites.

"Island in the Sky"

11/30/36–4/3/37—Mickey and Goofy buy an airplane and discover an island in the sky filled with marvelous inventions and run by a brilliant scientist named Dr. Einmug. Peg-Leg Pete appears as a spy after Einmug's atomic power formula.
Plotted and penciled by Floyd Gottfredson, written by Ted Osborne, inked by Ted Thwaites.

"In Search of Jungle Treasure"

4/5–8/7/37—Captain Churchmouse invites Mickey, Minnie, and Goofy on an African treasure hunt. Spooks, Captain Churchmouse's pet gorilla from "Mickey Mouse Sails for Treasure Island," reappears, as does the team of Peg-Leg Pete and Eli Squinch.
Plotted and penciled by Floyd Gottfredson, written by Ted Osborne, inked by Ted Thwaites.

"The Monarch of Medioka"

8/9/37–2/5/38—Mickey is kidnaped because he is the exact double of King Michael XIV of Medioka. His job is to take the king's place and restore the economy of Medioka while the spendthrift king is sent on vacation. This serial was banned in Yugoslavia because censors thought it too closely paraleled local political conditions.
Plotted and penciled by Floyd Gottfredson, written by Ted Osborne and Merrill de Maris, inked by Al Taliaferro (8/9–8/14) and Ted Thwaites.

"The Mighty Whale Hunter"

2/7–7/1/38—Mickey and Goofy enlist on a whaling vessel in search of a killer whale named Old Barney. There's a reward for the whale's capture and Peg-Leg Pete is out to beat Mickey to it. The plot is based on "The Whalers" (1938).
Plotted and penciled by Floyd Gottfredson, written by Merrill de Maris, inked by Ted Thwaites and Bill Wright [?].

"The Plumber's Helper"

7/2–12/10/38—Mickey loses all his money in a stock crash and is forced to go to work as an apprentice to a very shady plumber named Joe Piper.
Plotted and penciled by Floyd Gottfredson, written by Merrill de Maris, inked by Ted Thwaites and Bill Wright [?].

"Mickey Mouse Meets Robinson Crusoe"

12/12/38–4/13/39—Walt Disney casts Mickey in a new movie, which becomes a real adventure with

Robinson Crusoe and Friday after the opening sequence. Mickey is drawn with round eyes containing pupils for the first time in the daily strip in this story, based on the cartoon "Mickey's Man Friday" (1935).
Plotted and penciled by Floyd Gottfredson, written by Merrill de Maris, inked by Ted Thwaites and Bill Wright.

"Unhappy Campers"

4/14–5/19/39—Mickey takes his nephews and Goofy on an accident-prone camping trip.
Plotted by Floyd Gottfredson, penciled by Floyd Gottfredson (4/14, 4/15, 5/15–5/19) and an unknown artist, possibly Tom Woods (4/17–5/13), inked by Ted Thwaites and Bill Wright.

"Mickey Mouse Outwits the Phantom Blot"

5/20–9/9/39—A mysterious criminal dressed totally in black baffles and almost kills Mickey with a series of fiendish traps. The most baffling

part of the mystery is that the Blot only steals a certain brand of cheap cameras.
Plotted and penciled by Floyd Gottfredson, written by Merrill de Maris, inked by Ted Thwaites and Bill Wright.

"The Miracle Master"

9/11/39–1/13/40—Mickey buys an old lamp that turns out to be of the magic variety, complete with a very strange genie. When his attempts backfire to help the residents of his town with the genie's magic, he retreats to Genieland and his efforts there meet with the same lack of success. The idea for the genie and the magic lamp came from the cartoon "Pluto's Dream House" (1940).
Plotted and penciled by Floyd Gottfredson, written by Merrill de Maris, inked by Ted Thwaites and Bill Wright.

"An Education for Thursday"

1/15–4/20/40—Friday, last seen in the "Robinson Crusoe" adventure, sends Mickey his "almost-twin brother" Thursday for an education. Unfortunately, Thursday proves to be uncontrollable by anyone except Goofy.
Plotted and penciled by Floyd Gottfredson, written by Merrill de Maris, inked by Ted Thwaites and Bill Wright.

"The Bar-None Ranch"

4/22–8/17/40—When Mickey finds out the dude ranch Minnie and Clarabelle are visiting is being terrorized by a bandit with a wooden leg, he and Goofy head west to the rescue. The villain turns

out to be Peg-Leg Pete, of course, but this time he's using advanced technology to outwit pursuit and Mickey is stumped by an invisible wall around Pete's hideout.
Plotted and penciled by Floyd Gottfredson (possibly penciled by Manuel Gonzales from 6/17–6/21), written by Merrill de Maris, inked by Ted Thwaites and Bill Wright.

"Mickey Mouse, Bellhop Detective"

8/19–12/21/40—Mickey gets a job as a bellhop at a resort hotel plagued by ghosts and a missing $10,000.
Plotted and penciled by Floyd Gottfredson, written by Merrill de Maris, inked by Ted Thwaites and Bill Wright.

"The Land of Long Ago"

12/23/40–4/12/41—Mickey and Goofy fly to a tropical island that time forgot at the request of Professor Dustibones. Their job is to capture a dinosaur and bring it back to civilization.
Plotted and penciled by Floyd Gottfredson, written by Merrill de Maris, inked by Bill Wright.

"Love Trouble"

4/14–7/5/41—Mickey gets a rival for Minnie's affections in the person of Montmorency Rodent, a high society rat. The cartoon "Mickey's Rival" (1936) influenced the plot.
Plotted and penciled by Floyd Gottfredson, written by Merrill de Maris, inked by Bill Wright.

"Mickey Mouse, Supersalesman"

7/7–10/4/41—Under pressure from Minnie to settle down, Mickey takes a job as third assistant art director with the Hot Flash Publicity Agency. The firm is in financial trouble and Mickey has to land a big account to save the day.
Plotted and penciled by Floyd Gottfredson, written by Merrill de Maris, inked by Bill Wright.

"The Mystery at Hidden River"

10/6/41–1/17/42—Clarabelle disappears while on vacation in the North Woods so Mickey takes a job as a lumberjack to investigate. His boss is Peg-Leg Pete, going under the alias of Pierre de la Pooch and sporting a new store-bought leg. Sylvester Shyster reappears for the first time since 1934.
Plotted and penciled by Floyd Gottfredson, written by Merrill de Maris, inked by Bill Wright.

"The Gleam"

1/19–5/2/42—The town is startled by a series of jewel robberies, the work of an international master of hypnotism.
Plotted and penciled by Floyd Gottfredson, written by Merrill de Maris, inked by Bill Wright.

"Goofy and Agnes"

5/4–8/15/42—Goofy buys a friendly lion from the circus, but the city passes an anti-lion law that would require him to destroy Agnes.
Plotted and penciled by Floyd Gottfredson, written by Bob Karp (5/4–5/16) and Dick Shaw, inked by Bill Wright.

"The Black Crow Mystery"

8/17–11/21/42—To help the World War II defense effort, Mickey and Goofy take jobs on a farm that is plagued by a series of mysterious fires set by a giant black crow.
Plotted and penciled by Floyd Gottfredson, written by Dick Shaw, inked by Bill Wright.

"Goofy's Car"

11/23–11/28/42—These strips are a week-long series of gags based on the premise that Goofy thinks his car has been stolen.
Plotted and penciled by Floyd Gottfredson, written by Dick Shaw, inked by Bill Wright.

Gag-a-day strips—11/30–12/12/42

Written by Dick Shaw, penciled by Floyd Gottfredson, inked by Bill Wright.

"Working to Win"

12/14–12/23/42—Mickey takes a job at an airplane factory manned almost entirely by women.
Plotted and penciled by Floyd Gottfredson, written by Dick Shaw, inked by Bill Wright.

Gag-a-day strips—12/24/42–5/29/43

Written by Dick Shaw, penciled by Floyd Gottfredson (except 1/13, 1/14, 1/19, 1/21, 2/5, 2/9, 2/13, 2/19, 3/5, 3/12, 3/15 penciled by Bill Wright), inked by Bill Wright (12/24/42–1/?/43 and 1/13, 1/14, 1/19, 1/21, 2/5, 2/9, 2/13, 2/19, 3/5, 3/12, 3/15) and Dick Moores (1/?–5/29, except the dates listed above).

"Mickey Mouse's Wild Holiday"

5/31–6/26/43—Mickey takes his nephews on a camping trip where they're bothered by a persistent Indian trader and his pet bear.
Plotted and penciled by Floyd Gottfredson, written by Dick Shaw, inked by Dick Moores.

"The Nazi Submarine"
6/28–7/17/43—At the request of Chief O'Hara Mickey infiltrates a black market gasoline ring run by Nazi spies.
Written by Bill Walsh, penciled by Floyd Gottfredson, inked by Dick Moores.

"Mickey Mouse On a Secret Mission"
7/19–10/23/43—Mickey pilots "The Bat," an experimental flying wing, to Nazi Germany.
Written by Bill Walsh, penciled by Floyd Gottfredson, inked by Dick Moores.

"The 'Lectro Box"
10/25/43–2/5/44—Mickey accidentally invents an electronic box that can work miracles. The

villain of the story is Dr. Grut, a mad scientist who turns people into "aberzombies."
Written by Bill Walsh, penciled by Floyd Gottfredson, inked by Dick Moores.

"Pluto the Spy Catcher"
2/7–2/19/44—Pluto stows away on a battleship and becomes a hero—accidentally.
Written by Bill Walsh, penciled by Floyd Gottfredson, inked by Dick Moores.

Gag-a-day strips—2/21–3/11/44
Written by Bill Walsh, penciled by Floyd Gottfredson, inked by Dick Moores.

"The War Orphans"
3/13–4/15/44—Mickey gives shelter to three war orphans menaced by Nazis.
Written by Bill Walsh, penciled by Floyd Gottfredson, inked by Dick Moores.

"The Pirate Ghostship"
4/17–7/15/44—Mickey and Pluto sign on board a tuna fishing boat, but it's blown off course into the "Haunted Latitudes," where they are picked up by a 17th century pirate ship captained by Greatbeard, a man who looks exactly like Peg-Leg Pete.
Written by Bill Walsh, penciled by Floyd Gottfredson, inked by Dick Moores.

Gag-a-day strips—7/17–7/29/44
Written by Bill Walsh, penciled by Floyd Gottfredson, inked by Dick Moores.

"The World of Tomorrow"
7/31–11/11/44—Mickey receives an invisible cloak in the mail that transports him into the postwar world, a technologically advanced society that

is free of crime except for Peg-Leg Pete and his army of mechanical men.
Written by Bill Walsh, penciled by Floyd Gottfredson, inked by Dick Moores.

"The House of Mystery"
11/13/44–1/27/45—Maximillian Mouse, Mickey's least favorite uncle, leaves him a detective agency. Upon taking it over he discovers a connection

between his uncle and a mysterious young woman named Drusilla who he finds bricked up inside a wall.
Written by Bill Walsh; penciled by Floyd Gottfredson (11/13–12/2, 12/18–12/23, 1/1–1/8, 1/22–1/27), Paul Murry 12/4–12/16, and Dick Moores (12/25–12/30, 1/9–1/20); inked by Dick Moores.

Gag-a-day strips—1/29–3/3/45
Written by Bill Walsh; penciled by Dick Moores (1/29–1/31, 2/7, 2/8, 2/10, 2/13, 2/15, 2/17), Floyd Gottfredson (2/1–2/3, 2/5, 2/6, 2/9, 2/19, 2/20, 2/23, 2/24, 2/27, 2/28), and Paul Murry (2/12, 2/14, 2/16, 2/21, 2/22, 2/26, 3/1–3/3); inked by Dick Moores.

"Billy, the Mouse"
3/5–6/16/45—Mickey heads west, accompanied by a jive-talking Indian, to help out his cousin Carrie. There, disguised as Billy, the Mouse, he joins a gang of rustlers.
Written by Bill Walsh, penciled by Floyd Gottfredson, inked by Dick Moores.

Gag-a-day strips—6/18/45–2/23/46
Written by Bill Walsh; penciled by Floyd Gottfredson (6/18–7/24, 7/26, 7/30, 8/1–10/1, 10/8, 10/9, 10/16–11/30, 12/3–2/9, 2/16, 2/18), Paul Murry (7/25, 7/27, 7/28, 10/2–10/6, 10/10–10/15, 12/1, 2/23[?]), and Manuel Gonzales (2/11–2/15, 2/19–2/22); inked by Dick Moores (6/18–1/5) and Bill Wright.

"Mickey's Great-Grandfather"
2/25–3/2/46—Albermarle Mouse, "Injun fighter, explorer, sojer o' fortune," comes for a visit.
Written by Bill Walsh, penciled by Manuel Gonzales, inked by Bill Wright.

Gag-a-day strips—3/4–3/9/46
Written by Bill Walsh, penciled by Paul Murry, inked by Bill Wright.

Note: from March 11, 1946, through September 20, 1947, the *Mickey Mouse* daily strip featured 39 "continuities," all approximately two weeks in length. Because of the shortness of the stories, most were little more than a series of gags on a single theme. They are listed and titled below for the sake of completeness, but individual synopses would be pointless.

"The New Girlfriend"—3/11–3/23/46
Written by Bill Walsh, penciled by Manuel Gonzales (3/11–3/16) and Paul Murry, inked by Bill Wright.

"Mickey's Mini-Plane"—3/25–4/13/46
Written by Bill Walsh; penciled by Bill Wright (3/25, 3/26), Manuel Gonzales (3/27–3/30, 4/3, 4/4, 4/11–4/13), Paul Murry (4/1, 4/2, 4/5, 4/6), and Floyd Gottfredson (4/8–4/10); inked by Bill Wright.

"The Mystery Next Door"—4/15–5/4/46
Written by Bill Walsh, penciled by Floyd Gottfredson (4/15, 4/17, 4/22–5/4) and Manuel Gonzales (4/16, 4/18–4/20), inked by Bill Wright.

"Mickey Mouse in Gangland"—5/6–5/18/46
Written by Bill Walsh, penciled by Floyd Gottfredson, inked by Bill Wright.

"The Sunken Treasure"—5/20–6/1/46
Written by Bill Walsh, penciled by Floyd Gottfredson, inked by Bill Wright.

"Trailer Trouble"—6/3–6/15/46
Written by Bill Walsh, penciled by Floyd Gottfredson, inked by Bill Wright.

"Aunt Marissa"—6/17–6/29/46
Written by Bill Walsh, penciled by Floyd Gottfredson, inked by Bill Wright.

"The Candidate"—7/1–7/13/46
Written by Bill Walsh, penciled by Floyd Gottfredson, inked by Bill Wright.

"The Little Genius"—7/15–7/27/46
Written by Bill Walsh, penciled by Floyd Gottfredson, inked by Bill Wright.

"Goofy's Boat Race"—7/29–8/10/46
Written by Bill Walsh, penciled by Floyd Gottfredson, inked by Bill Wright.

"Goofy, the Kid"—8/12–8/24/46
Written by Bill Walsh, penciled by Floyd Gottfredson, inked by Bill Wright.

"Eviction"—8/26–9/7/46
Written by Bill Walsh, penciled by Floyd Gottfredson, inked by Bill Wright.

"Goofy's Rocket"—9/9–9/21/46
Written by Bill Walsh, penciled by Floyd Gottfredson, inked by Bill Wright.

"Mickey's Menagerie"—9/23–10/5/46
Written by Bill Walsh, penciled by Floyd Gottfredson, inked by Bill Wright.

"The Cure for Hiccups"—10/7–10/19/46
Written by Bill Walsh, penciled by Floyd Gottfredson, inked by Bill Wright.

"Thanksgiving Dinner"—10/21–11/2/46
Written by Bill Walsh, penciled by Floyd Gottfredson, inked by Bill Wright.

"The Search for Geeko"—11/4–11/16/46
Written by Bill Walsh, penciled by Floyd Gottfredson, inked by Bill Wright.

"The Talking Dog"—11/18–11/30/46
Written by Bill Walsh, penciled by Floyd Gottfredson, inked by Bill Wright.

"Arctic Adventure"—12/2-12/14/46
Written by Bill Walsh, penciled by Floyd Gottfredson, inked by Bill Wright.

"Morty's Escapade"—12/16-12/28/46
Written by Bill Walsh, penciled by Floyd Gottfredson, inked by Bill Wright.

"The Fiendish Cat"—12/30/46-1/11/47
Written by Bill Walsh, penciled by Floyd Gottfredson, inked by Bill Wright.

"Truant Officer Mickey"—1/13-1/25/47
Written by Bill Walsh, penciled by Floyd Gottfredson, inked by Bill Wright.

"Goofy's Inheritance"—1/27-2/8/47
Written by Bill Walsh, penciled by Floyd Gottfredson, inked by Bill Wright.

"Mickey the Icky"—2/10-2/22/47
Written by Bill Walsh, penciled by Floyd Gottfredson, inked by Bill Wright.

"Pluto's Amnesia"—2/24-3/8/47
Written by Bill Walsh, penciled and inked by Floyd Gottfredson.

"Peg-Leg Pete Reforms"—3/10-3/22/47
Written by Bill Walsh, penciled and inked by Floyd Gottfredson.

"Home Movies"—3/24-4/5/47
Written by Bill Walsh, penciled and inked by Floyd Gottfredson.

"Shutterbug Mickey"—4/7-4/19/47
Written by Bill Walsh, penciled and inked by Floyd Gottfredson.

"The Boxer"—4/21-5/3/47
Written by Bill Walsh, penciled and inked by Floyd Gottfredson.

"Mickey's Strange Flower"—5/5-5/17/47
Written by Bill Walsh, penciled and inked by Floyd Gottfredson.

"The Midget Racer"—5/19-5/31/47
Written by Bill Walsh, penciled and inked by Floyd Gottfredson.

"Mickey's Pet Shop"—6/2-6/14/47
Written by Bill Walsh, penciled and inked by Floyd Gottfredson.

"Mickey's Helicopter"—6/16-6/28/47
Written by Bill Walsh, penciled and inked by Floyd Gottfredson.

"Pluto's Trial"—6/30-7/12/47
Written by Bill Walsh, penciled and inked by Floyd Gottfredson.

"The Spook Specialist"—7/14-7/26/47
Written by Bill Walsh, penciled and inked by Floyd Gottfredson.

"Mickey Writes the Songs"—7/28-8/9/47
Written by Bill Walsh, penciled and inked by Floyd Gottfredson.

"Horace's Nerves"—8/11-8/23/47
Written by Bill Walsh, penciled and inked by Floyd Gottfredson.

"The Skyscraper Adventure"—8/25-9/6/47
Written by Bill Walsh, penciled and inked by Floyd Gottfredson.

"The Foundling"—9/8-9/20/47
Written by Bill Walsh, penciled and inked by Floyd Gottfredson.

"The Man of Tomorrow"
9/22-12/27/47—Mickey and Goofy discover a strange creature, supposedly from the year 2447, in a dark cavern. His name is so hard to pronounce that Mickey christens the little fellow "Eega Beeva" and takes him home, where scientists

examine Eega and decide he is "the man of tomorrow." From this story until mid-1950, Eega takes Goofy's place as Mickey's sidekick.
Written by Bill Walsh, penciled and inked by Floyd Gottfredson.

"Mickey Makes a Killing"
12/29/47-2/7/48—Eega Beeva can predict the future by eating pigeon feathers so Mickey uses his friend's power to make a killing in the stock market.
Written by Bill Walsh, penciled and inked by Floyd Gottfredson.

"Pflip the Thnuckle-Booh"
2/9-2/28/48—Mickey enters Eega's strange dog in a neighborhood pet show.
Written by Bill Walsh, penciled and inked by Floyd Gottfredson.

"The Santa Claus Bandit"
3/1-4/5/48—Chief O'Hara enlists Mickey's aid in tracking down a bandit who breaks into banks and **leaves** money.
Written by Bill Walsh, penciled and inked by Floyd Gottfredson.

"The Kumquat Question"
4/6-4/28/48—Somebody steals Eega Beeva's kumquats, the only food that keeps him alive.
Written by Bill Walsh, penciled and inked by Floyd Gottfredson.

"The Atombrella and The Rhyming Man"
4/30-10/9/48—Eega invents an umbrella that can withstand an atomic blast. The Rhyming Man, "a master spy, well bred but mean" is out to steal it.
Written by Bill Walsh, penciled and inked by Floyd Gottfredson.

"An Education for Eega Beeva"
10/11-12/25/48—Eega's strange ways get him into so much trouble that Mickey is determined to teach him how to act. Before the plan can succeed, however, Eega is arrested and forced to face a sanity hearing.
Written by Bill Walsh, penciled and inked by Floyd Gottfredson.

"Pflip's Strange Power"
12/27/48-3/5/49—Mickey discovers that Eega's dog can detect when someone is lying, but when the pooch is poisoned, Eega turns to Peg-Leg Pete for help and is drugged into betraying Mickey.
Written by Bill Walsh, penciled and inked by Floyd Gottfredson.

"Be-Junior and the Aints"
3/7-8/6/49—Eega builds a rocket ship that takes him and Mickey to the planet Be-Junior, inhabited by a race of faceless humans and large, intelligent animals called Aints.
Written by Bill Walsh, penciled and inked by Floyd Gottfredson.

"Itching Gulch"
8/8-10/22/49—Mickey and Eega visit a ghost town while on vacation out west and discover the fountain of youth.
Written by Bill Walsh, penciled and inked by Floyd Gottfredson.

"The Syndicate of Crime"
10/24/49-1/28/50—Pflip displays yet another strange power: the ability to sniff out criminals. With his help Mickey and Eega open a detective

agency and track down an international crime syndicate headed by Mr. Lamb.
Written by Bill Walsh, penciled and inked by Floyd Gottfredson.

'The Moook Treasure"
1/30-7/8/50—Mickey buys an old children's book and discovers a clue to the fabulous Moook treasure. Peg-Leg Pete appears as a Communist spy and reveals that he has always been one.
Written by Bill Walsh, penciled and inked by Floyd Gottfredson.

"Mousepotamia"
7/10-9/30/50—Eega Beeva goes home to the center of the earth and Mickey gets involved with Gus and Jaq, the **Cinderella** mice, who inform him that he is the heir to the throne of Mousepotamia, a strangely medieval country ruled with an iron fist by the Iron Mask.
Written by Bill Walsh, penciled by Floyd Gottfredson, inked by Floyd Gottfredson and possibly Bill Wright (8/21-9/9, 9/25-9/30).

"Land Beneath the Sea"
10/2–12/30/50—On his way home from Mousepotamia via balloon Mickey crashes at sea where he is rescued by a nutty scientist who gives

him a belt that enables him to breathe underwater. He discovers an undersea kingdom where it is a capital crime to be impolite.
Written by Bill Walsh, penciled by Floyd Gottfredson, inked by Floyd Gottfredson and possibly Bill Wright (11/20–23, 12/4, 12/5).

"Tzig-Tzag Fever"
1/1–3/24/51—Mickey is bitten by the Tzig-Tzag fly and contracts a fatal disease. To find a cure he travels to the heart of Africa in search of the Golden Goddess.
Written by Bill Walsh, penciled and inked by Floyd Gottfredson.

"Dry Gulch Goofy"
3/26–6/23/51—Mickey and Goofy go to Hollywood where Goofy becomes a cowboy star.
Written by Bill Walsh, penciled and inked by Floyd Gottfredson.

"The Ghost of Black Brian"
6/25–10/20/51—Mickey and Goofy rent a haunted house and make friends with Black Brian, an incompetent ghost, until the evil Dr. Doom finds a way to control ghosts and starts a spirited crime wave.
Written by Bill Walsh, penciled and inked by Floyd Gottfredson.

"Uncle Wombat's Tock Tock Time Machine"
10/22/51–1/19/52—Goofy's uncle invents a time machine that transports the boys to the American revolution, ancient Rome, and a future world ruled by talking flowers.
Written by Bill Walsh, penciled and inked by Floyd Gottfredson.

"The Midas Ring"
1/21–4/19/52—Mickey does a favor for a Gypsy who gives him a ring that causes money to seem to gravitate to him—much to his regret.
Written by Bill Walsh, penciled and inked by Floyd Gottfredson.

"The Isle of Moola-La"
4/21–10/2/52—Mickey discovers the map and a deed to an island that has the world's best black pearl beds. His quest is aided by a magician named Khan Dhoo and hindered by Peg-Leg Pete.
Written by Bill Walsh, penciled and inked by Floyd Gottfredson.

"Hoosat from Another Planet"
10/3/52–2/28/53—While Mickey and Goofy are prospecting for uranium they discover a mechanical man named Ohm-Eye and a group of aliens

from the planet Unnlax, on Earth to mine bleerium, an almost magical element.
Written by Bill Walsh, penciled and inked by Floyd Gottfredson.

"Mickey's Dangerous Double"
3/2–6/20/53—A dangerous criminal who looks like Mickey has perpetrated a crime wave and Mickey is blamed for the robberies.
Written by Bill Walsh, penciled and inked by Floyd Gottfredson.

"The Magic Shoe"
6/22–10/28/53—Mickey travels to Ireland in search of a cure for his persistent hiccups. The people of the village he visits have all been turned into birds by the King of the Little People and Mickey is taken to the Leprechaun's magic kingdom.
Written by Bill Walsh, penciled by Floyd Gottfredson (6/22–9/26, 10/5–10/28) and Bill Wright (9/28–10/3), inked by Floyd Gottfredson and possibly Bill Wright (6/22–6/26, 6/29–7/2, 7/4, 7/14–7/16, 8/10–8/21, 9/7–9/10, 9/24–10/3) and Dick Moores (7/27–7/30).

"Mickey Takes Umbrage"
10/29/53–1/30/54—Mickey becomes the caretaker of Umbrage, a college-educated gorilla.
Written by Bill Walsh, penciled by Floyd Gottfredson, inked by Floyd Gottfredson and possibly Bill Wright (1/25–1/28).

"A Fatal Occupation"
2/1–5/15/54—Mickey is taken to the center of the earth to the underground land of Concavia to become the next king, a job that comes with a short life expectancy for the man on the throne.
Written by Bill Walsh, penciled and inked by Floyd Gottfredson.

"The Kid Gang"
5/17–9/18/54—Leavenworth Lee, an escapee from a reform school, turns up in a basket on Mickey's doorstep. Soon the orphan is kidnaped and forced to join a gang of criminal children.
Written by Bill Walsh, penciled and inked by Floyd Gottfredson.

"Uncle Gudger"
9/20–12/31/54—Mickey's uncle comes for an extended visit bringing some odd friends and a lifetime's worth of accumulated junk.
Written by Bill Walsh, penciled and inked by Floyd Gottfredson.

"Dr. X"
1/1–5/20/55—Goofy disappears only to turn up later as the brilliant Dr. X, with no memory of his former life.
Written by Bill Walsh, penciled and inked by Floyd Gottfredson.

"Pluto in Love Trouble"
5/21–6/25/55—Pluto rescues a sick Pekinese who turns out to be a terror when she recovers.
Written by Bill Walsh, penciled by Floyd Gottfredson, inked by Floyd Gottfredson and possibly Manuel Gonzales (6/6–6/18).

"Li'l Davy"
6/27–10/4/55—Li'l Davy, a pint-sized version of Davy Crockett, arrives in town with Jiminy Crockett and insists that everyone live like a frontiersman. By this time the strip had come full circle and the storyline was once again a collection of gags based on a single theme. From October 5th on, the format was strictly gag-a-day.
Written by Bill Walsh, penciled and inked by Floyd Gottfredson.

THE SUNDAY PAGES

"Dan, the Dogcatcher"
7/31–8/28/32—Pluto is hunted by a dogcatcher named Dan (Peg-Leg Pete's exact double) because Mickey can't afford to buy a dog license. The dollar Mickey borrows from Judge Barker to pay for the license is referred to in the 9/4/32 page. *Written and penciled by Floyd Gottfredson, inked by Ted Thwaites.*

"Mickey's Nephews"
9/18–11/6/32—Morty and Ferdie Fieldmouse debut in the strip as they arrive for an extended visit. The Sunday pages making up this sequence are basically a series of gags based on Mickey's inability to handle the high-spirited boys. *Written and penciled by Floyd Gottfredson, inked by Ted Thwaites.*

"The Lair of Wolf Barker"
1/29–6/18/33—Mickey and the gang visit Uncle Mortimer's ranch out west where Minnie is kidnaped by Wolf Barker, head of a gang of cattle rustlers. In an interesting attempt at continuity,

Wolf Barker later reappears in one panel of the 7/9/33 Sunday as one of Mickey's nightmares. *Written by Ted Osborne, penciled by Floyd Gottfredson, inked by Al Taliaferro (1/29–2/19, 4/16–4/30) and Ted Thwaites (2/26–4/9, 5/7–6/18).*

"Rumplewatt the Giant"
3/11–4/29/34—Mickey tells a group of kids a fairy tale about the time he defeated a giant, rescued the goose that lays the golden eggs, and freed Minnie from an enchantment that had turned her into a butterfly. The story was inspired by the 1933 cartoon, "Giantland." *Written by Ted Osborne, penciled by Floyd Gottfredson, inked by Ted Thwaites.*

"Tanglefoot Pulls His Weight"
5/6–6/3/34—Mickey decides to go into the delivery business using his horse Tanglefoot to pull a milk wagon, an ice wagon, etc. *Written by Ted Osborne, penciled by Floyd Gottfredson, inked by Ted Thwaites (5/6) and Al Taliaferro.*

"Dr. Oofgay's Secret Serum"
6/17–9/9/34—The gang goes on a camping trip to the lake and meets goofy Dr. Oofgay. He has a serum that will turn wild animals tame and vice-versa, and he tests it on Horace. *Written by Ted Osborne, penciled by Floyd Gottfredson, inked by Al Taliaferro.*

"Foray to Mt. Fishflake"
12/9/34–1/20/35—Mickey, Minnie, Horace, and Clarabelle climb Mt. Fishflake to win the $1,000 prize offered by the Gazopp Liniment Co. *Written by Ted Osborne, penciled by Floyd Gottfredson, inked by Ted Thwaites.*

"The Case of the Vanishing Coats"
2/17–3/24/35—The tailor shop belonging to Donald's "Uncle" Amos is being robbed so the boys hide there at night in an attempt to catch the thief. *Written by Ted Osborne, penciled by Floyd Gottfredson, inked by Ted Thwaites.*

"Hoppy the Kangaroo"
7/28–11/24/35—Uncle Mortimer sends Mickey a kangaroo from Australia and Mickey enters him

in a boxing match with a gorilla owned by Peg-Leg Pete. This continuity was based on "Mickey's Kangaroo" (1935). *Written by Ted Osborne, penciled by Floyd Gottfredson, inked by Ted Thwaites.*

"Mickey's Rival"
1/5–1/26/36—Another Mortimer, this time a practical joking rat, enters the strip as a rival for Minnie's affection. *Written by Ted Osborne, penciled by Floyd Gottfredson, inked by Ted Thwaites.*

"Helpless Helpers"
3/1–3/22/36—Mickey, Donald, and Goofy make an attempt to help Minnie with some home repairs. *Written by Ted Osborne, penciled by Floyd Gottfredson, inked by Ted Thwaites (3/1, 3/8) and Al Taliaferro.*

"The Robin Hood Adventure"
4/26–10/4/36—Mickey shrinks himself with reducing fluid and goes through the pages of a book to the world of Robin Hood where he becomes a very unmerry Merry Man. *Written by Ted Osborne, penciled by Floyd Gottfredson, inked by Ted Thwaites (4/26–7/5, 7/26, 8/2, 8/30) and Al Taliaferro (7/12, 7/19, 8/9–8/23, 9/6–10/4).*

"The Ventriloquist"
10/11–11/8/36—Mickey learns how to throw his voice and goes around the neighborhood making people think that Pluto can talk. *Written by Ted Osborne, penciled by Floyd Gottfredson, inked by Al Taliaferro.*

"Sheriff of Nugget Gulch"
5/16–10/24/37—Mickey and Goofy visit Uncle Mortimer's ranch again and gain reputations as desperados until they capture Pancho Malarky, the gunman really behind all the trouble. *Written by Ted Osborne, penciled by Floyd Gottfredson, inked by Al Taliaferro.*

"Service With a Smile"
3/6–4/3/38—Mickey and Goofy try to manage a gas station owned by Uncle Jasper. *Written by Ted Osborne, penciled by Floyd Gottfredson, inked by Al Taliaferro.*

"The Brave Little Tailor"
8/28–11/27/38—As in the "Robinson Crusoe" daily adventure, Mickey is cast as an actor in a movie, an adaptation of the 1938 cartoon short of the same name. "Mac" McCorker is once again Mickey's director. *Written by Merrill de Maris, penciled by Floyd Gottfredson (8/28, 9/4, 11/27) and Manuel Gonzales, inked by Ted Thwaites.*